TORTURED NOBLE

the story of

Leo Tolstoy

TORTURED NOBLE
the story of
Leo Tolstoy

Neil Heims

MORGAN REYNOLDS

PUBLISHING
Greensboro, North Carolina

WORLD WRITERS

Charles Dickens

Jane Austen

Ralph Ellison

Stephen King

Robert Frost

O. Henry

Roald Dahl

Jonathan Swift

Leo Tolstoy

TORTURED NOBLE: THE STORY OF LEO TOLSTOY
Copyright © 2007 by Neil Heims

Library of Congress Cataloging-in-Publication Data

Heims, Neil.
    Tortured noble : the story of Leo Tolstoy / by Neil Heims.
        p. cm.
    Includes bibliographical references and index.
    ISBN-13: 978-1-59935-066-0
    ISBN-10: 1-59935-066-1
    1. Tolstoy, Leo, graf, 1828-1910. 2. Authors, Russian--19th century--
Biography. I. Title.
    PG3385.H38 2007
    891.73'3--dc22
    [B]
                                        2007011389

Printed in the United States of America
First Edition

for Ted Solotaroff

Contents

Leo Tolstoy
(Courtesy of Topham/The Image Works)

one

The Peasant Count

On June 10, 1881, a middle-aged Russian aristocrat, a count, dressed like a peasant, with a pack on his back and a staff in his hand, wearing shoes made of tree bark, bid farewell to his disapproving family and set out on a pilgrimage. He planned to walk from his ancestral estate to the monastery at Optina-Pustyn. Two servants followed discreetly behind, carrying money and a suitcase of clean linen.

The wealthy aristocrat dressed as a peasant, off on a religious pilgrimage, was not merely an eccentric and guilt-ridden wealthy landowner. Leo Tolstoy was the most revered writer in Russia—perhaps the most revered writer in the world. His epic novel of the Napoleonic wars, *War and Peace*, is ranked with the work of Homer and Shakespeare. His other great novel, *Anna Karenina,* is a probing study of marriage, social class, romantic love, and spiritual quest, filled with an astounding variety of human experiences. Many critics and scholars list both of Tolstoy's great works among the ranks of the greatest novels ever written.

Throughout his life, Tolstoy jumped between the contradictory forces of his character. His spiritual hunger warred with his sensual nature. He grabbed at pleasure with a ferocious appetite then pushed it away in disgust. He enjoyed the privileges of his wealth, most of which he had inherited, while being aware of the deep poverty and disparities around him. He sought glory but was acutely aware of its transience. In his youth he had spent days losing great sums of money at card tables, and nights in drunken carousing and trying to satisfy his sexual craving. He followed these episodes of debauchery with

Tolstoy dressed as a peasant *(Courtesy of Hulton Archive/Getty Images)*

days of self-loathing and self-reproach, and resolutions never to do it again. But there would always be a next time.

In the late 1870s, Tolstoy finally experienced the spiritual rebirth he had longed for most of his life. He embraced

Christianity and set out to renounce his former pleasures and compulsions. Always a man of extremes, he then turned against everything he had ever been and known. The count wanted to be a peasant. The novels and stories that had placed him in the pantheon of great authors were rejected as disgraceful wastes of time. His wealth and property became burdens. He even decided that his wife and children were obstacles blocking his path to truth and honesty.

Tolstoy's life story is strange, painful, but also deeply intriguing and exhilarating. How did a man who produced so much work of such value become obsessed with a need to erase and denigrate all he had created? What did Tolstoy believe he was achieving with his acts of self-obliteration? What set him on this journey seeking self transcendence at all costs?

Leo Nikolayevich Tolstoy, the son of Nikolai Ilyich Tolstoy, was born on August 28, 1828, at the family estate of Yasnaya Polyana. (The "Nikolayevich," in his name, like the "Ilyich" in his father's, is called a patronymic. It indicates that Leo Tolstoy was the son of Nikolai. Nikolai's patronymic indicates he was the son of Ilya.)

His mother, Marya Nikolayevna Volkonskaya, died when Tolstoy was only twenty-three months old. The rest of his life Tolstoy remembered her as a shadowy ideal of perfection. The only picture he had of her was a silhouette done in profile.

Marya Nikolayevna Volkonskaya had been the delight of her widowed father, Prince Volkonsky, who taught her physics, mathematics, geometry, and geography. She was proficient in Russian and fluent in French, German, Italian, and English. She also played the piano and was respected for

Tolstoy's house in Yasnaya Polyana *(Courtesy of Novosti/TopFoto/Image Works)*

her steadiness of character and her gift as a storyteller. She was, however, considered to be a homely girl, and it was not expected she would ever marry. Her marriage with Nikolai Ilyich Tolstoy was not a love match.

Nikolai Ilyich Tolstoy had joined the army in 1812, when he was seventeen, and fought against the French armies led by Napoleon Bonaparte when they invaded Russia. In 1813, Nikolai was captured by the French and force-marched to Paris, where he was held a prisoner of war until 1814, when Russian troops freed him. Nikolai remained in the army until 1819, retiring with the rank of lieutenant colonel and going to live on his father's estate in Kazan. His father was the governor of Kazan, and Nikolai entered the civil service. Despite the prestige and privileges the family seemed to enjoy, when Nikolai's father died in 1820 he left only debt, the consequence of years of living beyond his means.

Nikolai Ilyich Tolstoy, Leo's father, fought against the French army during Napoleon's *(above)* invasion of Russia in 1812. Tolstoy would later use the Napoleonic Wars as the backdrop for his epic novel, *War and Peace.*

The solution to Nikolai Tolstoy's financial difficulties lay in marrying a wealthy woman. In 1822, he resigned from the civil service, married Princess Marya Nikolayevna Volkonskaya, and settled with her on her family estate at Yasnaya Polyana, which would be Tolstoy's home throughout his life.

Although it began as a marriage of convenience, Nikolai and Marya formed a strong bond and lived together happily. She bore five children; Leo was the youngest of four brothers. His sister Marya was the baby of the family. When Marya died in 1830, the children were cared for by Nikolai's mother, Pelageya Tolstaya, and two aunts, Alexandra Ilyinichna Osten-Saken and Tatanya Alexandrovna Yergolski.

Tolstoy's grandmother was an autocrat who delighted in luxury. When she went out to the hazel wood to pick hazelnuts, she traveled seated in her yellow cabriolet. The servants lowered the branches of the trees to her. Tolstoy loved one of her servants, an old blind man named Lev Stepanich, who was a natural storyteller. He liked to sit by his grandmother's side in her room and listen to Stepanich's tales.

His aunt, Alexandra, who also lived at Yasnaya Polyana, was a refugee from an insane and violent husband who had assaulted her several times and had once tried to cut her tongue out with a razor. Alexandra was a pious Christian and spent her time reading *The Lives of Saints* and giving hospitality to the religious pilgrims—called *bogomolitzi*—who trekked past Yasnaya Polyana as they wandered ceaselessly from monastery to holy place.

The woman Leo was closest to was Tatanya. He called her his aunt, but she was actually his father's second cousin. Tatanya had been adopted by his grandmother when she and her sister were orphaned as children. As a girl, although she was in love with Nikolai, she accepted his marriage of convenience to Princess Marya with humility. But her willingness to make self-sacrifices endowed her with a stubborn pride. After Marya died, she refused Nikolai's offer of marriage but promised always to be a mother to his children. Leo loved her like a mother, and she remained a model of devoted love and self-sacrifice his entire life.

Until Leo was five, these three women, and the house servants, made up most of Tolstoy's world. When he turned five he was taken from the upstairs company of women and sent downstairs to be among his brothers. He quickly became close to them. They all boasted imaginative qualities and became comrades in what Nikolai, the eldest brother, called the "brotherhood of ants." (This was a pun. The word *muraveinye*, which means "ant" in Russian, sounds like *Moravskiye*, or

Moravian, a religious sect. Rather than Moravian Brethren, they were brother ants.) The brothers built hideaways under two chairs where they huddled together and made up stories about a world governed by love and goodness. Older brother Nikolai told them of a magic wand that was buried, a green stick, under a tree on a hillside in the forest of Zakaz nearby. There was a magic word on the stick that had the power to bring peace, brotherhood, and happiness.

Leo's world as a young aristocrat was dependent on the peasants. When he was a child, peasants in Russia were called serfs, essentially slaves. But little Leo did not see them as property. They were the people who loved and cared for him, and he loved them in return.

Leo's first encounter with the injustice of serfdom made a deep, painful impression that left him with strong feelings of guilt. He was out for a walk with his tutor when he saw his friend, Kuzma, the assistant coachman, being taken to the stables to be flogged. He was horrified at the punishment and in awe at Kuzma's calm submission to it. When he told his Aunt Tatanya what he had seen, he was mortified when she told him that he had the power, because he was a young master, to have prevented the beating. Leo was shocked that he had more power than the grown man and felt he was responsible, even if indirectly, for the punishment.

Leo's first tutor, Fyodor Ivanovich Rössel, a German immigrant who had been a shoemaker, was not a very learned man, but was kind and affectionate. He taught the children German, filled them with moral precepts, and encouraged them to write. Among Leo's papers are two pages with lines ruled in pencil, part of a magazine the brothers put together. An entry signed by Leo and dated 1835 reads: "The eagle is

When Leo was nine years old, he moved with his family to Moscow so his brothers could attend the university there. (*Library of Congress*)

the king of birds. They say about it that a certain boy began to tease it; it grew angry and pecked at him." At age seven, Leo was already fascinated by the conflict between daring actions and their sometimes dangerous consequences.

In 1837, when Leo was nine, his father moved the family to a large, expensive rented house in Moscow so the eldest son, Nikolai, then fourteen, could prepare for the entrance exams to the university. In the city Leo took long walks with his tutor. He also began spending his time alone making up stories and writing them down. His first story, written inside a blue notebook he had sewn together himself, was called "The Children's Library." It went on for eighteen pages before breaking off incomplete:

> In the town of P. [it began] there lived an old man ninety years of age who had served under five emperors, who had seen more than one hundred battles, who held the rank of

colonel, who had ten decorations paid for in blood for he had
ten wounds and walked on crutches having only one leg. . . .
He had five children. . . .

In 1837, the course of the Tolstoy family was tragically altered. Nikolai Ilyich Tolstoy had not been well for some time. He drank too much, suffered a recurring cough, and often spat up blood. His physical problems were aggravated by stress brought on by money troubles. Then, late in June, while on a business trip to Tula, he suffered a stroke and fell dead in the middle of the street. Because his money and papers were missing when his body was found, it was suspected by some, although never proven, that the two servants traveling with him had murdered and robbed him.

Nine-year-old Leo was confused by his father's death and had trouble accepting it. He kept thinking he had seen his father on the street. In church, when a requiem mass was offered for his father's soul, Leo had the feeling his father's death made him important. He suddenly felt like the center of attention, which he undoubtedly was. He was now an orphan without an inheritance. Despite the circumstances, he enjoyed being the focus of attention, although he felt guilty about enjoying it. "I was continually preoccupied with myself: I was always conscious, rightly or wrongly, of what people thought of me, and worried about the feelings I inspired in those around me, and this spoiled all my pleasure," he wrote later in his *Confession*.

His aunt Alexandra became the guardian of the Tolstoy children, but her religious fervor absorbed most of her attention. Leo's grandmother, old, ill, and bedridden, was also incapable of looking after the children or of dealing with their financial difficulties.

Tatanya took upon herself the burden. In order to cut down expenses, the first thing she did was find a smaller, five room apartment.

One ongoing expense was the children's education. There were eleven tutors plus a dancing master. Spending money on Leo's education did not seem to be a good investment. His new instructor, a Frenchman named Prosper St. Thomas—a much less amiable man than Rössel had been—wrote that Leo was neither willing nor able to work. He complained that Leo could not understand arithmetic and made no effort to memorize facts. But St. Thomas did recognize something special in the boy and described him as "a young Molière."

The tutor's praise of Leo's writing ability, however, did not stop him from taking severe measures to make him behave. He often berated the boy and called him a "good-for nothing." At one point he ordered Leo to kneel before him. When Leo refused, St. Thomas pushed him to his knees, humiliating the boy. Another time St. Thomas locked Leo in a dark closet.

After their grandmother's death, the two older boys, Nikolai and Sergey, remained in Moscow in an even smaller apartment to prepare for the university entrance exams. Leo, Dmitry, and Masha returned to Yasnaya Polyana to stay with Tatyana.

In August 1841, when their guardian, Aunt Alexandra, died, the guardianship of the family passed not to Tatyana, but to Alexandra's younger sister, Pelageya. Pelageya held a long-standing grudge against Tatyana, who had been an old flame of Pelageya's husband, even rejecting his offer of

Tolstoy's estate at Yasnaya Polyana is located about 112 miles south of Moscow.

marriage at one point. Pelageya moved the family away from Yasnaya Polyana, and from Tatyana, to her estate in Kazan. The move was not made totally out of spite, however; there was also the need to economize. Plus, there was a university in Kazan.

Around this time, Leo began a rigorous course of physical training and began to develop, at his own initiative, some self-discipline. At the tender age of ten he had endured the death of both parents, the loss of three other important figures in his life, and moving from one household to another. He was convinced that if he were to survive he must be strong and learn how to endure suffering, even, if possible, learn to let the suffering make him stronger.

Leo's regimen was designed to strengthen his body. He practiced vigorous gymnastics, but the training was not limited to exercise. He lashed his naked back until he cried from the pain and, beginning the pattern of indulgence and denial

Tolstoy as a young man

that lasted his entire life, he sometimes wallowed in self-indulgence and tried to live for the pleasure of the moment. He would go without doing his lessons or would spend days stretched across his bed reading adventure novels, gorging himself with gingerbread.

Leo also began to torture himself with unanswerable questions about life and death, pleasure and pain, whether God existed and, most importantly, what was his role in it all? Was he important? The more conscious he became of the world and concerned about fundamental issues, the more he became self-conscious. He entered adolescence as a very shy boy convinced that he was hopelessly ugly and ungainly. However, photos of young Tolstoy reveal this his opinion of himself was more self-conscious than accurate.

two

Youth

Leo Tolstoy was not eager to enter the university at Kazan. He was still a lazy student. But Aunt Pelageya wanted him to become a diplomat, maybe even an aide-de-camp to the Tsar. He had no plans of his own so, with the help of tutors, he began to study for the entrance examinations to be admitted to what was called the Faculty of Oriental Languages, which was the prerequisite program for entering the diplomatic service. He took the exams and, although his performance in the religion, German, and English examinations was strong, he failed the history, geography, statistics, and Latin exams and was denied admission.

After a second attempt at the entrance exams, in the autumn of 1844, Leo was admitted. But getting in and staying in were two different matters.

Tolstoy chose to focus on his social life instead of his studies while attending Kazan University.

Much more alluring than his classes were the temptations of student life. Tolstoy wore his student uniform, resplendent with its gold buttons, including a sword on his left hip, with pride, and traveled in his own horse and carriage. He also took up smoking and cut classes so often that by midterm he was subject to expulsion. Not wanting to give up the student life, even if doing a student's work was not congenial to him, Leo switched his major. Instead of training to be a diplomat, he decided to study law. The Faculty of Jurisprudence was a department well known for the laxity of its standards.

Even in the easier major, Leo performed poorly on midyear examinations. He did manage to discipline himself enough to do well on finals, although his real focus remained on his social life in Kazan. He shared an apartment with his brothers Sergey and Dmitry (Nikolai had graduated and gone into the army), went to the theater and to balls, drank, gambled at cards, and performed in theatricals. However, despite all the care he took to make sure his fingernails were well manicured, to dance, bow, and converse with easy grace, to pronounce his French well, and, most importantly to affect a casual air of indifference to everything, Leo was awkward, stiff, and

Tolstoy as a student

shy. Women usually found him boorish and unattractive. For female companionship, he frequented women who were not admitted into respectable drawing rooms, which led to several bouts of gonorrhea. Although he often reproached himself for his lax lifestyle and went through intense periods of tormented penitence, he always returned to it.

Leo's brothers took him to a brothel when he was fourteen. After the act, he later wrote, he wept at the woman's bedside. Even so, he continued to frequent brothels until he was married. His rationale was that going to brothels was necessary to maintain his health and to prevent a disturbing sexual tension from building up inside him.

Leo often felt spiritual and intellectual affection for some of his male friends. He shared his thoughts in lengthy conversations with Dmitry Dyakov, and felt a warmth for him he later described as having a sensuous component. "I will never forget the night, when we [Leo and Dyakov] left Pirogovo," he wrote. They sat beside each other in a sleigh. "I wanted to kiss him and weep. There was voluptuousness in this feeling. . . . Why it occurred . . . it is impossible to decide, for my imagination did not paint lubricious pictures. On the contrary, I had a great aversion to them."

Nikolai Gogol

Although Leo's father had left him nearly penniless, there was an inheritance from his mother. In 1847, he became the master of Yasnaya Polyana, his mother's home, along with 5,400 acres of land and 350 male serfs and their families. He broke off his studies, left Kazan, and assumed the responsibilities that being lord of Yasnaya Polyana imposed upon him.

Leo was only nineteen. He had done poorly in school—instead of giving him a grade on his midterm exam, his Russian history professor had written "extremely lazy"—and had so far lived a dissipated and thrill-seeking lifestyle. But, even at such a young age, he had a conviction that his life should be justified by a commitment to something more honorable than simply servicing his personal needs and wants. Although he had neglected his schoolwork, Leo had not totally neglected his education. He read deeply—French and English novels, political science, the Bible, particularly the New Testament, and philosophy.

He was soaking up influences that would shape him as a writer. He read the Russian masters and contemporaries, including Nikolai Gogol, Ivan Turgenev, Mikhail Lermontov, and Alexander Pushkin. He read the philosophers, Hegel, Voltaire, and Rousseau. Rousseau, who said humans were all born free but chose to live out lives in captivity, was particularly influential. *Emile*, Rousseau's novel about education, was a foundation for the philosophy of freedom in education Leo would attempt to put into practice when he opened a school for peasant children at Yasnaya Polyana.

three
Becoming a Writer

It seemed that Tolstoy never wanted to be where he was at the time, whether it was at school in Kazan or at Yasnaya Polyana. Within a month of his arrival in Moscow in 1848 he had become dissatisfied. He stayed busy visiting the best drawing rooms in the city and entertaining visitors at his apartment, but the incessant socializing did not keep him from becoming bored and disgusted with the city and his life there. Although Tolstoy said he wanted to get back to the country, he moved to St. Petersburg in early 1849.

St. Petersburg excited him for a while. He had "many more acquaintances here than in Moscow; and they are of a much higher quality," he wrote Sergey. He decided to go back to school in order to enter government service. After cramming for a week he passed the entrance examinations for criminal and civil law, but once admitted he did not buckle down and study. Instead, he reignited his passion for

In 1849, Tolstoy moved to St. Petersburg. *(Library of Congress)*

gambling and before long had lost so much money he had to write to Sergey and ask him to sell a woodlot and some horses to pay off gambling debts.

By spring, thoroughly disgusted with himself again, Tolstoy returned to Yasnaya Polyana, where he could reduce his expenses. He intended to study for a civil service examination, but in November he obtained a post in the Chancellery of the Tula Assembly of Nobles. The job required little work, and he again spent most of his time gambling, drinking, and frequenting brothels.

When he had again temporarily exhausted his appetite for city life, Tolstoy returned to Yasnaya Polyana at the beginning of the summer of 1850. There he practiced piano and

During his younger years, Tolstoy was a compulsive gambler and often had to call on his friends and family to pay his gambling debts. This photo depicts young men of that era. *(Courtesy of The Bridgeman Art Library)*

wrote a treatise on "The Fundamental Principles of Music and Rules for Its Study." He resumed doing daily calisthenics and wrote a treatise on that called "On Gymnastics."

Soon after obtaining a post in Tula, Tolstoy took a leave of absence and never returned. He left the countryside again for Moscow, this time "with three aims, (1) to gamble; (2) to marry; (3) to obtain a post." Gamble he did, but he failed to find a wife or obtain a post. He frequented plenty of drawing rooms where he flirted with the married hostesses, and caroused in gypsy haunts and brothels. As always, he was torn between desire and disgust and kept a record of self-

Before his marriage, Tolstoy would visit prostitutes to sate his sexual appetite. *(Courtesy of Alinari/Art Resource)*

reproach detailing his sins. This moral introspection was in many ways his apprenticeship as an author. He was on the verge of beginning to apply himself seriously to writing fiction. In Moscow in 1850 he jotted down a plan for a story of gypsy life and began a story about his childhood. *Childhood,* his first published work, would appear in 1852.

Writing did not absorb all his energy. There was still time for dissipation and the wearying cycle of self-abuse and self-abnegation. When his brother Nikolai, who had been serving with the army in the Caucasus for four years, visited Moscow, Tolstoy agreed to accompany him back to the

Caucasus. Perhaps the change would help him free himself from the cycle.

The Caucasus region is a relatively small but rich and diverse region of towering mountains, wide valleys, thick forests, and rivers lying some 1,200 miles south of Moscow between the Black Sea to the west and the Caspian Sea to the east. Culturally it is a region where Muslim and Christian cultures met and mixed. The several ethnic and religious groups in the region have lived together for centuries, sometimes at peace and sometimes not.

When Tolstoy arrived on May 31, 1851, he said that he felt the presence of God in the lofty beauty of the mountains. This epiphany intensified his longing to renounce his corrupt behavior, and for a few days he believed he was beginning a new life. Then he lost nearly a thousand rubles at cards, got drunk, and visited a prostitute.

Tolstoy volunteered to participate in a raid on a Chechen village, hoping to learn more about warfare and the psychology of killing.

Unlike Moscow, Petersburg, or Kazan, the Caucasus was a war zone. Tolstoy had not arrived as a soldier, but when Major General A. I. Baryatinski led a raid on a Chechen village, he invited Tolstoy to come along as a volunteer. Tolstoy later reproached himself for feeling fear during the raid, but his commander admired his courage under fire and suggested he enlist. Still looking for ballast, Tolstoy joined the army in 1852. He served in the Russian army until the end of 1856. He joined because he had nothing better to do, because the adventure excited him, and because he wanted to understand killing. He wanted to know "under the influence of what feeling one soldier kills another." Although he served only four years, his army experience would help to shape him into the man and the writer who would eventually write *War and Peace* and *Anna Karenina*.

Tolstoy spent two months in Tiflis before going into the army undergoing mercury treatment, which before antibiotics was the only treatment for venereal disease. He also found time to complete the first part of *Childhood*. He was still not sure if he had writing talent but believed enough in himself and what he had written to send it to the poet N. P. Nekrasov, editor of *The Contemporary*, although he signed the manuscript with only his initials. Nekrasov praised the work for "the simplicity and the reality of [the] subject" and accepted it for publication. He also told Tolstoy not to "hide behind initials." *Childhood* was published in the autumn of 1852 and was a great success. After reading it, the prominent writer Ivan Turgenev wrote to Nekrasov that Tolstoy had a "sure gift."

Tolstoy read the reviews of his first book with "unbelievable joy." Success encouraged him to continue writing, and he became more productive. A story called "The Raid," *Boyhood*, the continuation of *Childhood*, the three of what came to be called the *Sevastopol Sketches*, "A Wood-Felling," "The Novel of a Russian Lord," and "Memoirs of a Billiard-Maker" were written between 1853 and 1856. He also began another work, *The Cossacks*, which he put aside and did not finish until 1863.

four
War

Nicholas I

In 1853, Tsar Nicholas ordered the invasion of the Ottoman Empire of Turkey. Nicholas claimed his action was necessary to defend Orthodox Christians living in the Ottoman Empire, but in actuality it was an attempt to expand Russian borders. In November, the Russian Black Sea fleet defeated the Turkish fleet at the Battle of Sinope off the coast of Sevastopol. This sea battle was the first engagement of what became known as the Crimean War after England and France entered as allies with Turkey in an effort to check Russian expansion into the Mediterranean and the Middle East. Both the British and the French had their own imperialistic plans for those regions.

Tolstoy's essay "Sevastopol in December 1854" emphasized heroism and endurance in the face of wartime adversity, and garnered acclaim from literary critics and Tsar Alexander II.

By the time war had begun, Tolstoy had tired of the army and submitted a request to resign, but his request was denied. He then applied to become a commissioned officer and asked to be transferred to the battle zone in Crimea, a peninsula on the Black Sea. Although he would later write about the politics and grand design of war in *War and Peace*, his aim in asking to be sent there was to see how war was fought at the front, as well as to study the character of fighting men.

Tolstoy took and passed the officer's exam and was promoted to the rank of ensign. After a visit to Yasnaya Polyana, where he was reunited with his three brothers, he left for Bucharest in March 1854. He remained there for a short time until he was transferred to Sevastopol, the seaside city in the Crimea where the war was raging.

This Franz Roubaud painting, titled *The Siege of Sevastopol*, depicts the Russian invasion of Turkey.

He was still working on *The Cossacks*, but he quickly turned out three Sevastopol sketches that were immediately published. *The Cossacks*, an unfolding tale of human relationships filled with diverse characters, conflicting cultures, and transformations of consciousness, was an ambitious project perhaps outside of his skills at this early stage of his career. The Sevastopol stories are like snapshots, and writing them helped Tolstoy to develop his eye for detail and ability to convey deep emotional depth and feeling in simple language. "Sevastopol in December 1854," for example, is a work of tremendous power. Rather than writing in the first person, Tolstoy uses second person—"you"—throughout, encouraging the reader to make the writer's perceptions his or her own.

You enter the large Assembly Hall. As soon as you open the door you are struck by the sight and smell of forty or fifty amputation and most seriously wounded cases, some in cots but most of them on the floor. Do not trust the feeling that checks you at the threshold, it is a wrong feeling. Go on, do not be ashamed of seeming to have come to look at the sufferers, do not hesitate to go up and speak to them. Sufferers like to see a sympathetic human face, like to speak of their sufferings, and to hear words of love and sympathy. You pass between the rows of beds and look for a face less stern and full of suffering, which you feel you can approach and speak to.

"Where are you wounded?" you inquire hesitatingly and timidly of an emaciated old soldier who is sitting up in his cot and following you with a kindly look as if inviting you to approach him. I say "inquire timidly" because, besides strong sympathy, sufferings seem to inspire a dread of offending, as well as a great respect for him who endures them.

"In the leg," the soldier replies, and at the same moment you yourself notice from the fold of his blanket that one leg is missing from above the knee. . . .

You begin now to understand the defenders of Sevastopol, and for some reason begin to feel ashamed of yourself in the presence of this man. You want to say too much, in order to express your sympathy and admiration, but you can't find the right words and are dissatisfied with those that occur to you. And so you silently bow your head before this taciturn and unconscious grandeur and firmness of spirit—which is ashamed to have its worth revealed.

"Sevastopol in December 1854" expresses the horror of war, but is not an indictment of war and the leaders who wage war. It is an account of the heroism of endurance and the heroism of submission, rather than the heroism of action. When Tsar Alexander II read it he was overwhelmed and ordered it translated into French. According to legend, he

Tsar Alexander II *(Library of Congress)*

even sent word to the front telling Tolstoy's commanders to "guard well the life of that young man."

Honored by the Tsar and lauded by the St. Petersburg literary critics, Tolstoy now realized he could have a career as an author. This tempted his vanity, but he soon realized that having a career as a writer would come at a price too dear for his conscience. He could not write without conviction. The next Sevastopol sketch would make that clear.

In May 1855, Tolstoy became the commander of a battery of mountain gunman. The sketch he drew from this experience did not earn the Tsar's approval. Instead, it was heavily censored before publication. Although the work reflected his continuing commitment to the men who fought in the Tsar's war, his disgust at the vanity, futility, and brutality of war penetrated the story. The early Sevastopol sketch had made every man in it a hero, the second had none.

> Look at this ten-year-old boy in an old cap . . . with shoes on his stockingless feet and nankeen trousers held up by one brace. . . . [H]e . . . has been walking about the valley . . . looking with dull curiosity at . . . the corpses that lie on the ground and gathering the blue flowers with which the valley is strewn. Returning home with a large bunch of flowers he holds his nose to escape the smell that is borne towards him by the wind, and stopping near a heap of corpses gazes for a long time at a terrible headless body that lies nearest to him. After standing there some time he draws nearer and touches with his foot the stiff outstretched arm of the corpse. The arm trembles a little. He touches it again more boldly; it moves and falls back to its old position. The boy gives a sudden scream, hides his face in his flowers, and runs towards the fortifications as fast as his legs can carry him.

If the first Sevastopol sketch is objective reportage, the second is charged with Tolstoy's moral perspective:

> The people around do not, on seeing what they have done . . . fall repentant on their knees before Him who has given them life and laid in the soul of each a fear of death and a love of the good and the beautiful, and do not embrace like brothers with tears of joy and gladness.

On the contrary: "The white flags are lowered, the

engines of death and suffering are sounding again, innocent blood is flowing and the air is filled with moans and curses."

Tolstoy then steps outside his role as narrator and speaks directly to the readers, as he did later in his famous novels and religious writings:

> There, I have said what I wished to say this time. But I am seized by an oppressive doubt. . . .
>
> Where in this tale is the evil that should be avoided, and where the good that should be imitated? Who is the villain and who the hero of the story? All are good and all are bad.
>
> The hero of my tale—whom I love with all the power of my soul, whom I have tried to portray in all his beauty, who has been, is, and will be beautiful—is Truth.

For the first time in his writing, Tolstoy states what would become his overwhelming conviction in his work, and life. For him, the pursuit of truth was the pursuit of an ideal of perfection.

When he had arrived in Sevastopol, Tolstoy was disgusted with himself. He saw his life as aimless, without purpose or passion for anything worthwhile. He felt a "wound deep in my heart," whose "ache" he did not know "how to soothe." Military service and the experience of war did not soothe that aching wound any more than dissipation and debauchery. His time at the front only made his wounded heart ache more, but it allowed him to see that the same wound existed in everyone. His army years did give him a deeper range of feeling and understanding, as well as experiences that served him as a writer, and deepened his belief that his life must be guided by his convictions.

As his time in the army was ending, Tolstoy wrote in his diary that, "the aim of [life] is welfare and the ideal is virtue." Everything he believed in was opposed to what he found in the army and in war. "Soldiers are animals taught to bite everybody," he wrote soon after leaving the army, after viewing Napoleon's tomb at *Les Invalides* in Paris in 1856. Rather than participate in the violence and hatred that set men and nations against each other, he wanted to seek out the means to promote peace, loving-kindness, and concord. At the beginning of March 1855 he wrote in his diary that he was "capable of devoting my life" to "found[ing] a new religion that fits human evolution, a religion of Christ but stripped of faith and mysteries, a practical religion which does not promise future beatitude but gives beatitude on earth."

five

After the War

When Tolstoy arrived in St. Petersburg in November 1855, he was preceded by his new fame as a successful young writer. He was an immediate favorite in society and introduced himself to the older writer Ivan Turgenev, who offered him a place to stay in his house. This began a long-term love/hate relationship between the two writers. Turgenev was a bon vivant—someone with cultivated, refined tastes—and an aesthete. Tolstoy was offended by the older man's seeming lack of concern about social issues and his frivolity. Aesthetically they were different as well. Turgenev believed in the purity of literature and thought a commitment to art was the highest possible human achievement. As he aged, Tolstoy would frequently come to think of authorship as an unworthy pursuit.

As Turgenev introduced him to St. Petersburg's literati, Tolstoy became increasingly bored and irritated by their debates about the mean- ing and the uses of art and whether to identify them- selves with Western European values or with a Slavic tra- dition. Boredom soon drove Tolstoy back into his old ways. Turgenev wrote to a friend that Tolstoy spent a great deal of his time "painting the town red! Orgies, gypsy dance halls, cards all night, and then he sleeps like the dead until two o'clock."

When Tolstoy returned to Yasnaya Polyana he was not much more settled than he had been before joining the army. He did have

ВЕЗЕНБЕРГЪ и КⁿО   С.ПЕТЕРБУРГЪ.

Tolstoy maintained a long relationship with Russian writer Ivan Turgenev. *(Library of Congress)*

some projects he wanted to undertake, including finding ways to improve the lot of the serfs on his estate by granting them their freedom and land to live on and cultivate.

Freeing the serfs was a popular idea in the 1850s. When Tsar Nicholas I died and Alexander II acceded to the imperial throne in 1855, there was a great deal of hope that he would free the serfs. In March of 1856, Alexander addressed the nobles in Moscow and warned them the time was approaching when the serfs would have to be freed and it would "therefore be much better for it to come from above than from below." Alexander wanted the nobility independently to emancipate their serfs. That way they could direct the change themselves instead of running the risk of an uprising.

At Yasnaya Polyana, Tolstoy gathered his serfs together and told them that God had put into his mind the conviction to set them free. If he could free them legally he would, he said, but that was not possible under current Russian law. He then proposed turning over twelve acres of land to each family. In return, they would pay him a nominal fifteen rubles a year for thirty years. This way each family could own and farm its own piece of land. Tolstoy could not just give the land to the peasants because he was in debt as a result of his youthful spending and had mortgaged his estate. He asked the peasants to think about his proposal and to talk it over. He then suggested that after three days they ought to meet again so they could tell him what they had decided. If they did not like his proposal they could then suggest changes.

When they met again Tolstoy was shocked to discover that the serfs did not trust his motives. There were rumors circulating that the tsar himself was planning to emancipate them, which was true. He did in 1861. The peasants believed that the tsar would give them all the land that now belonged to the nobility, which was not true. Because of this misunderstanding about the tsar's future plans, Tolstoy's serfs rejected his plan.

Tolstoy was disappointed that the serfs rejected his plan, but it also clarified his understanding of the class situation in Russia and intensified his feeling about it. "The despotism of the landowners has already engendered despotism in the peasants," he wrote to his friend, the president of the Department of the Laws in Petersburg, Count D. N. Bludov. "When they told me at the meeting that I should give them all the land outright, and I said that I should be left without my shirt, they laughed. . . . [I]t was impossible to blame them."

Tolstoy's other project after leaving the army was to find a wife. He was convinced this was essential for his peace of mind and physical well-being because he was torn apart by sexual desire that he could only satisfy in a manner he considered immoral. When his friend Dyakov suggested Valerya Vladimirovna Arsenev, who lived with her family at Sudakovo, a short distance away from Yasnaya Polyana, as a possible mate, Tolstoy began courting her. His impression of Valerya was not particularly favorable. He thought she was "without backbone and fire." Although she was "kind . . . her smile . . . is painfully submissive." To mark this inauspicious beginning he concluded a diary entry by noting, "Returned home and sent for the soldier's wife," in all likelihood his peasant mistress, Aksinya Bazykin.

The qualms that Tolstoy felt about asking Valerya to marry him characterized the rest of his short, half-hearted courtship. When it began to seem to her family that he was a serious suitor, he suddenly left for Moscow. From there he went on to St. Petersburg, where he continued to lead his old life of debauchery.

Whatever else was going on around him, for good or for bad, he continued to write. He also developed a sense of responsibility for other writers and helped to establish a charitable organization dedicated to supporting impoverished writers, the *Society for the Aid of Needy Authors and Learned Men.* One of the first beneficiaries of the society was the novelist Fyodor Dostoevsky who, unlike Tolstoy, was not a man of independent means.

Fyodor Dostoevsky

Tolstoy was wracked with guilt for courting a woman he knew he did not want to marry and did not hold in high esteem. His behavior towards her was "the reprehensible desire to inspire love." His unending bouts of lust followed by self-reproach, as well as the web of intrigues spun in Petersburg and Moscow society, continued to torment him. In this state of mind, after receiving his formal discharge from the army, he set out, on January 12, 1857, on a trip through Western Europe.

Tolstoy arrived in Paris at the *Gare du Nord* on February 9. The city dazzled him. He stayed at the elegant Hotel Meurice on the *rue de Rivoli,* and then rented a furnished apartment on the same fashionable street a few blocks to the west of the *Palais du Louvre* and a few doors away from an apartment Turgenev kept for his daughter, Paulinette, and her mother, his fickle mistress, the singer Pauline Viardot-Garcia. Turgenev took Tolstoy around to salons, the opera, museums, concerts, theater, and other parts of the sort of nether world Tolstoy later reproached himself bitterly for having frequented. He attended lectures at the Sorbonne and traveled with Turgenev to Dijon, where they shared a chilly hotel room.

Despite his hectic schedule Tolstoy kept writing while Turgenev, who was grieving over Pauline's capricious treatment of him, complained that he felt written out. After a quarrel sparked by Turgenev's dislike of a story he was writing, Tolstoy left Dijon and returned to Paris.

Now Paris began to disgust him. Visiting Napoleon's tomb, Tolstoy was suddenly filled with indignation. "This idealization of a malefactor," he noted in a diary entry on March 4, 1857, "is shameful." A week before, he had entered in his notebook, "Read a speech by Napoleon with unspeakable loathing. No one has understood better than the French that people worship insolence—a good punch in the face. The trick is to act with conviction; then everyone will step aside and even feel he is in the wrong. That is what I realized, reading Napoleon's speech." One of the major historical characters of *War and Peace* was taking shape for him.

The decisive event that forced Tolstoy to flee Paris, however, occurred early in April, when he saw a man guillotined. "I should have been less sickened to see a man torn to pieces before my eyes," he wrote to his friend, the Russian literary critic V. P. Botkin, "than I was by this perfected, elegant machine by means of which a strong, clean, healthy man was killed in an instant. . . . In the first case, there is no reasoning will, but a paroxysm of human passion; in the second, coolness to the point of refinement, homicide-with-comfort, nothing big. . . . And the awful crowd! A father was explaining to his daughter how this very painless and ingenious mechanism worked."

The day after seeing the public execution near the Place de la Bastille, Tolstoy left for Geneva, Switzerland, where he planned to meet his aunt, the Countess Alexandra Tolstoy. Ten years older than Tolstoy, Alexandra, a Lady-in-Waiting at the Russian court, was traveling with the Grand Duchess Marie as her children's companion. Tolstoy maintained a close friendship with Alexandra throughout his life, sometimes using her as a confidante and sometimes, especially in his later years when strong political and religious differences came between them, quarreling with her about politics and religion. Their mutual affection, however, never wavered. Even in his later years, she served as his emissary to the tsar's court, providing information when he needed it or intervening on his behalf—usually, through no fault of her own, without success.

After meeting in Geneva they traveled together through Switzerland, stopping at some of the famous resorts in the Alps. When Alexandra returned to Geneva, Tolstoy continued his excursions, backpacking with Sasha Polivanov, the eleven-year-old son of an acquaintance he made at the lakeside Swiss village of Clarens. Tolstoy described his delight at being out in the open in his *Travel Notes*. He loved "when the same air that you breathe makes the deep azure of the illimitable heavens; when you do not exult and rejoice alone in nature, but around you buzz and whirl myriads of insects; and beetles, clinging together . . . and all around you the birds pour forth song."

At Lucerne, Tolstoy stayed at the Schweizerhof Hotel. One evening he watched as a wandering Tyrolean minstrel sang outside the hotel, accompanying himself on guitar. A delighted crowd made up of the hotel's guests had come out onto the balconies to listen. When he finished playing, the minstrel held out his hat, but the crowd gave him nothing. The minstrel departed empty-handed. Incensed, Tolstoy ran after him, brought him into the hotel lobby and ordered a bottle of the best champagne. The waiter said the main salon was closed and tried to lead them to an employees' lounge, but, with aristocratic authority, Tolstoy insisted they be served in the main salon. The guests who had slighted the musician earlier, now, to Tolstoy's delight, were scandalized by his presence among them.

Tolstoy had planned to visit Holland and England after traveling through Switzerland, and then return home by way of Rome and Paris. But in Germany, at the resort spa of Baden-Baden, he succumbed to the roulette wheels and lost all his money—and then lost more money that he had borrowed from a Frenchman he met in Zurich. He wrote to Turgenev, to his Aunt Alexandra, and to several other friends for help. Turgenev, vacationing nearby at Sinzing, on the Rhine, came directly to Baden-Baden and rescued—and scolded—his difficult young friend. Tolstoy lost the money Turgenev gave him at the gaming table, too.

When he returned to Russia, whether he was in St. Petersburg, or Moscow, or on his estate at Yasnaya Polyana, Tolstoy was haunted by the same malaise and burdened with one overwhelming idea: death made life seem worthless. "Work, a small reputation, money. What for? Material enjoyment—also what for? Soon eternal night. It always seems to me that I shall soon die." His life had no purpose and he was bored, his time filled with vain pursuits—flirtations and false love affairs, promenades on the boulevards, and paying calls, including calls on Valerya and her family. One of the families he called on, in addition to Valerya's, was the Behrs. He discovered that, despite his ennui, he enjoyed the company of the three young Behrs daughters.

Tolstoy's sister Marya and her three children came to Moscow for the winter of 1857, and he spent evenings listening to Marya play piano for her guests. He took the children to the theater and wrote a story for them based on their adventures. When he returned to Yasnaya Polyana he hunted and on one occasion wrestled a bear that tore at his face. Tolstoy was saved by a peasant who beat the bear off with a stick. He continued his liaison with his peasant mistress, Aksinya Sakhorov Bazykin, "the soldier's wife," and formed a plan for planting trees in the district of Tula. He lobbied the government in Petersburg for permission to go ahead with the project, but nothing came of it.

He could not stop contrasting his aimless empty life as a Russian aristocrat to how his serfs lived. Although he took pains to fill his days, more often than not his activities seemed meaningless and left him unsatisfied. Despite their poverty and the narrowness of their world view—or was it, Tolstoy began to wonder, because of those things—the peasants were not plagued by the anguish he saw in himself and in other members of his class. The peasants seemed to live in harmony with their world, seeking nothing beyond what they had, and accepted death and suffering with equanimity.

Tolstoy's literary reputation, which had begun so promisingly, began to fade. His stories, "Lucerne," which drew on the incident at the Schweizerhopf with the Tyrolean minstrel, and "Albert," a story of a ruined musician who endures an unappreciative public ignorant of true art and the egotistical patron who attempts to rehabilitate him, were deemed failures. He had lost his allure. When he heard of Tolstoy's non-literary projects, Turgenev wrote, "What does he want to be—an officer, a farmer . . . a timber expert[?] . . . I fear . . . that he will throw the spine of his talent out of joint. In his Swiss tales a very pronounced curvature is already noticeable."

"My reputation has fallen," Tolstoy wrote in his diary. "Inwardly I felt terribly grieved; but now I'm calmer. I know that I have something to say and the strength to say it powerfully."

Despite his bravado in his diary, Tolstoy was not sure he wanted to say anything in literature. His idea of art increasingly rejected what he called "literature of accusation," the fashion of the day. "However great may be the importance of a political literature that reflects the temporary interests of society," he said in his induction address to the Moscow Society of Lovers of Russian Literature in February 1859, "there is another literature that reflects eternal and universal interests, the dearest and deepest feelings of the people, a literature accessible to . . . all peoples and all times, a literature without which no people has ever developed that had sap and strength."

He did not think his work reflected this sort of art. His short novel, *Family Happiness*, published three months after the speech, in May 1859, dealt with early love and marital relations inside the context of the corrupting influence of society. "Received *Family Happiness*. It's a

Tolstoy spent much of his life learning about and experimenting with different ways to educate children. *(Courtesy of Lebrecht Music and Arts/The Image Works)*

shameful abomination," he wrote. A hint of his dissatisfaction with the novel can be detected from his response to a request for a story from *The Reading Library*, a literary review:

> I'm not much use as a writer any more. . . . Now that I have become mature, life is too short for me to fritter it away making up books like the ones I write, which are a source of embarrassment to me afterwards. . . . [T]o write novels that are charming and entertaining to read, at thirty-one years of age! I gasp at the thought.

What he decided to do instead was to run a school at Yasnaya Polyana that would teach the children of the serfs and peasants reading, writing, arithmetic, religion, and geography. He wrote his friend B. N. Chicherin, "I am working at something that comes as naturally to me as breathing and, I confess with culpable pride, enables me to look down on what the rest of you are doing." He told I. P. Borisov, "I am swamped with work, and fine work it is. A far cry from writing novels!"

In the summer he took his pupils into the fields and they all labored together. He wrote copiously about education. He even began a magazine, called *Yasnaya Polyana,* dedicated to the subject of education. He became interested in doing research into the educational methods used in the supposedly enlightened countries of Western Europe. He left the school in the hands of one of the teachers he was training and set out for Europe, specifically Germany, to get a close-up look at how its schools operated.

There were other reasons to leave Russia. Tolstoy's relationship with his peasant mistress, Aksinya Bazykin, had become more of an emotional commitment than he had expected. "I am afraid when I see how attached to her I am," he confessed in his diary. "The feeling is no longer bestial but that of a husband for his wife." Yet she was not his wife, and he was not ready to make her his wife, and did not have the strength to end the relationship. Another reason for his trip was to visit his brother Nikolai, who was suffering from tuberculosis and taking treatment at a spa in the German city of Soden. His other brother Dmitri had died of tuberculosis in 1856.

On this, his second and last trip away from Russia, Tolstoy was accompanied by his sister Marya, her husband, and their three children. Marya, two years younger than Tolstoy, was anxious about her own health and that of her brother and children.

They left St. Petersburg on July 2, 1860, on a paddle-steamer. Three days later, after a rough passage and Tolstoy's face swollen with a bad tooth, they docked at Stettin and then went on by coach to Berlin. In Berlin they consulted a specialist who examined the adults and the children and found no signs of tuberculosis. Marya and her family left for Soden to see Nikolai, who was in the final stages of the disease. Tolstoy remained in Berlin and for ten busy days visited schools, museums, and a prison, where the new practice of solitary confinement had just been introduced. He attended lectures at the university on history and physiology, and, with a German student he met there, went to classes for workers and to a workers' meeting. He liked the openness of the workers' school but was distressed at the rote learning and punishments he witnessed in the children's schools. His notes, often written in bitter fragments, indicate his disgust: "Prayer for the king, cuff on the head, everything by heart, children terrorized and benumbed."

Not every experience was dispiriting. In Dresden, he visited the novelist Berthold Auerbach, who wrote stories about peasant life that expressed ideas about education similar to Tolstoy's. "All methods are sterile," Auerbach told Tolstoy. "Anybody can be a great teacher. It's the children who create the best teaching methods, together with their teacher." Tolstoy tried to put that philosophy into practice at Yasnaya Polyana—forcing nothing on the children and trying to learn how and what to teach from them.

Nikolai's health worsened, but Tolstoy still delayed going to Soden. Nikolai visited him instead in Kissingen and returned to the spa alone two weeks later. Tolstoy agonized over his brother's condition and his own inability to be of any "use to anyone." In a state of great uneasiness he had disturbing dreams, such as the nightmare he described in his diary on August 11: "Dreamed that I was dressed as a peasant and my mother did not recognize me." The next day, he wrote that he had caught a cold and "[a]ll day long I was obsessed by fear for my lungs." By the time he got to Soden, he expected to undergo treatments himself, but upon arrival he was feeling fine. Nikolai, however, was not, and the doctors recommended they take him to Hyères in the south of France.

There was nothing anyone could do; Nikolai died on September 20, 1860. "Nothing is worse than death," Tolstoy wrote soon after his brother's death to his friend, the lyric poet Afanasy Fet. "But when one reflects . . . that that is the end of all, then, there is nothing worse than life. Why strive or try," he complained, "since nothing remains?" At his brother's funeral, he again felt the desire to found a new religion dedicated to the teachings of Christ that did not postulate Christ as supernatural—a "practical" or "materialist" Christianity. He envisioned it as a code of behavior for living this life, not a dogma or doctrine of the afterlife. In the spirit of the story of the green stick Nikolai had told his brothers when they were children, it was about creating heaven on earth.

In the day's following his brother's death, Tolstoy felt "detached terribly from life. . . . I try to write, I force myself, and I can't do it. . . . I cannot attach enough importance to work to muster up the strength and practice it demands. . . . Nikolenka's death has hit me harder than anything I have ever experienced."

He was eventually able to shake himself out of the torpor: "Shilly-shallying, idleness, depression, thoughts of death. Must get out of this. Only one way: make myself work." "Invaded by a host of images and ideas, such as I have not had for ten years," he did set himself to work on *The Cossacks,* the story drawn from his experiences during his first year in the Caucasus, and on a novel that absorbed him off and on for years but which never really got anywhere, *The Decembrists,* about the aftermath of a failed uprising against the tsar that happened in December 1825. Although he never completed *The Decembrists*, it would eventually provide the first seeds for *War and Peace.*

Tolstoy remained in Hyères until the end of 1860, spending his days among the large population of consumptives. He seemed to feel as if they were "part of [his] family," that they "had some power over him," Marya wrote. Nikolai's passing had increased Tolstoy's anxiety about death. It also deepened his sense of emotional relationship—even of identity—with the rest of mankind. His terror of death and the apparent lack of meaning in life was driving him closer to developing his own philosophy of how to find some sort of salvation, one grounded in acting lovingly in the world as it is.

During this period of mourning, meditation, and writing at Hyères, Tolstoy also taught Marya's children and their friends. He gathered them round a large table and wrote with them or played piano for them and did gymnastics with them. He made a short excursion to Marseilles and brought back watercolors and taught them to draw.

He went to Marseilles to visit the state schools there. After seeing eight in a single day, he was distressed at the harsh discipline and rote learning, which he believed dead-ened both the intelligence and the spirit of the children. After visiting an orphanage, he wrote, "At the sound of the whistle, four-year-olds revolve around their benches like soldiers, raising and crossing their arms on command, and in strange, quavering voices, sing hymns to god and their benefactors."

Tolstoy contrasted this regimentation to the street life of the city: "The French are nearly all the things they believe they are," he noted, "ingenious, intelligent, sociable, open-minded and, it is true, civilized. Look at a thirty-year-old town laborer: he can write a letter with fewer mistakes than the children in school can, sometimes without any at all; he has some notions of politics, history and modern geography." "Where has he learned it all?" he asked. His answer: it was "spontaneous education. . . . School is not at school, but in the newspapers and cafés." These voluntary associations pro-vided "an unconscious education many times stronger than the compulsory one."

During the first four months of 1861, Tolstoy passed through Nice, Florence, Livorno, and Rome. In Paris, he reconciled with Turgenev. In London, he attended a session in the House of Commons, a lecture on education by Dickens, and met with Matthew Arnold—a poet, literary and social critic—who was also a professor of poetry at Oxford and an inspector of schools. Through Arnold Tolstoy saw how English schools were run. He also met the exiled Russian socialist and editor of the revolutionary journal *The Bell*, Alexander Herzen, who found Tolstoy "a good and innocent man," although he wondered why Tolstoy could "not think instead of acting as if he were still at Sevastopol, taking the position by assault." From London

Tolstoy went to Brussels, where he met the anarchist-socialist revolutionary Pierre-Joseph Proudhon, who had been exiled from France by Napoleon III. He was excited by Proudhon's belief that the idea of private property had to be abolished before people could live in universal freedom and equality.

On February 18, 1861, Tsar Alexander II abolished serfdom, a move that Tolstoy supported. Proudhon wrote to a friend that Tolstoy had referred to Alexander's declaration as "a real emancipation" and had said that "[w]e do not free our serfs with empty hands, we give them property along with liberty."

In an article written shortly after this meeting, Tolstoy corroborated Proudhon's impression of his optimism. "[A]s much as one can judge from a distance," he wrote, "Russian society now showed itself conscious of the fact that without education of the masses no governmental organization can be durable." However, he wrote to Herzen at the same time,

On February 18, 1861, Tsar Alexander II abolished serfdom. This painting by Sergei Ivanov depicts serfs leaving their landlord after being emancipated.

after receiving a report from his brother Sergey regarding the response of the peasants at Yasnaya Polyana to the emancipation: "Have you read the exact terms of emancipation? To my mind it is utterly futile verbiage. I have received two letters from Russia telling me that the muzhiks [peasants] are all dissatisfied. Before, they could hope that everything would turn out all right; now they know for certain that everything will be all wrong . . . and the whole thing is the work of the masters."

When Tolstoy returned to his estate, he was burdened with the responsibility of helping his former serfs adjust to emancipation. They were permitted by law to buy small plots of land on the estates of their former masters, but there were inevitable disputes. In order to handle these disputes, the position of Arbiter of the Peace was created, and the governor of Tula, the district in which Yasnaya Polyana was situated, named Tolstoy to the post, over the opposition of the nobility. His radical projects, like the school and his generous treatment of the peasants, even before their emancipation, made the nobles fear how far he would try land reform.

In January 1862, while Tolstoy was in Moscow, the fever to gamble overcame him and he lost a thousand rubles at Chinese billiards. In order to raise money to pay the debt, he went to the director of the *Russian Herald* and sold him the rights to his novel, *The Cossacks*, as yet unfinished, for a thousand rubles. Although he had been writing it off and on for nearly ten years, he promised to deliver it by the year's end. This turned out to be the motivation he needed, and he finally finished it. "When all is said and done," he wrote to Botkin, "this solution suits me down to the ground, for the novel, of which I'd written over half, would otherwise have been left to rot and finally been used to stuff the cracks in the windows."

Tolstoy left Moscow towards the end of the winter of 1862 in poor health. The Moscow air had not agreed with him, the old malaise about his purpose in life continued to torment him, and conflicts with the nobility over his decisions as arbiter of the peace were a constant strain. Increasingly his decisions were overturned by higher authorities. Ultimately he resigned his post.

Tolstoy was still searching for a suitable wife. He began to focus his attention, tentatively, on nineteen-year-old Lisa Behrs, the oldest of Lyubov Behrs's daughters. When her parents began to consider him a possible fiancé, he ceased his courtship and returned to Yasnaya Polyana, where his health continued to deteriorate. He developed a bad cough and was again fearful that he had contracted tuberculosis. He returned to Moscow to consult with Lyubov's husband, Dr. Behrs, who confirmed that his lungs were weak and advised that he go to Samara, a region southeast of Moscow, on the left bank of the Volga river, for a kumys treatment.

Kumys is a fermented and slightly carbonated mare's milk that was thought at the time to have restorative properties. Tolstoy relied on it several times throughout his life and considered it to be beneficial. Kumys was made by a nomadic tribe called the Bashkirs that lived on the steppes in Samara. Those who went for the cure lived among them in felt tents. "I shall read no more newspapers, receive no letters, forget what a book looks like, wallow on my back in the sun, drink kumys, gorge myself on mutton until I turn into a sheep myself, and then I'll be cured," Tolstoy wrote to a friend.

He arrived in Samara towards the end of May 1862 and

spent more than a month on the steppes with the Bashkirs drinking kumys, eating mutton, hiking, wrestling, running, astonishing his hosts with feats of bodily strength, and conversing with the elders. When he returned to Moscow at the end of July he was in good spirits and in good health. But he did not find things to be as he had expected. In the early morning of July 6, while he was in Samara, the police had raided Yasnaya Polyana. Exactly what prompted the raid is not known, but it was likely that one of the landowners offended by Tolstoy's support of the rights of the peasants

Tolstoy's study. Russian police raided Tolstoy's house and rifled through books and papers hoping to find subversive material. *(Library of Congress)*

sent a letter to the Moscow police saying that one of the university students working as a teacher at Tolstoy's school had distributed anti-tsarist tracts.

M. I. Shipov was first sent to investigate. Shipov was a drunkard, and when the police in Tula reported him to his superiors in Moscow he was arrested for being drunk on duty. In an attempt to gain clemency, Shipov made up stories. He reported that there was a group of radical students at Yasnaya Polyana, and that their identification papers, which all Russians were required to carry, were not in order. He also claimed that they had an illegal printing press and intended to print and distribute subversive literature. He described the main house as a suspicious building with secret doors and hidden stairways.

Shipov's report led to the raid. For several days the police occupied Yasnaya Polyana. They searched the house, rifled through Tolstoy's books and papers, read his diaries, and looked for incriminating material but came up with nothing. Tolstoy's Aunt Tatanya's nerves were strained by the intrusion, and the servants were frightened. An outraged Tolstoy wrote to his cousin, Alexandra, at court:

> The peasants have ceased to regard me as an honest man—a reputation it took me years to acquire—and are treating me as a criminal, an arsonist or counterfeiter who had to finagle his way out of a tight spot. . . . They think, 'That's enough of your speeches about honesty and justice. You almost got sent up yourself.' . . . And the landowners . . . are chortling with glee.

Finally, the government accepted that it did not have a case, and an order was sent in the name of the tsar not to prosecute Tolstoy. This was as close to an apology as he would get. The incident signaled the beginning of suspicion and surveillance of Tolstoy and his circle that would continue throughout his life—even at his funeral.

six
Marriage

When he returned to Yasnaya Polyana from Europe, Tolstoy's desire to get married was stronger than ever. In a letter he had written to Sergey from Brussels about the family of one of his frequent hosts, Prince Dondukov-Korsakov, the vice-president of the Academy of Sciences, his interest was obvious. He noted there were "two daughters ill and another aged fifteen; as you can see, there is no material for matrimony here." He realized he was not prime husband material, either. "My last remaining teeth are crumbling to bits," he remarked. Regardless, "my spirits are high," he wrote to Marya while asking her to arrange a marriage with a woman he had met in Hyères, Katerina Alexandrovna, a niece of the Princess Golitsin. Then, as usual, at the last moment he had second thoughts.

When he finally achieved his goal of finding a suitable wife it was at the Behrs household, but not, as everyone expected, with the elder sister, Lisa. This time he was interested in the middle daughter, Sonya.

Various women in the Behrs family had occupied Tolstoy's romantic thoughts over the years. Dr. Behrs's wife, Lyubov Islenyev, had three brothers who had been his childhood friends. As a boy, he had been in love with Lyubov—she was three years older than Tolstoy—and once, jealous that she was paying more attention to another boy, he had pushed her off a balcony. She limped for days afterwards from the injury. Lyubov had married Dr. Andrey Behrs when she was sixteen and he thirty-four. After her marriage Tolstoy remained friendly with her and occasionally visited her and her growing family—she gave birth to eleven children, eight of whom lived, five sons and three daughters.

Sonya, the middle daughter, was eighteen when Tolstoy came to visit in 1862, after his trip to Europe. To Tolstoy, Sonya seemed to blend the best qualities of the three sisters. Lisa was beautiful and intelligent, with an interest in literature and philosophy, but also willful and melancholy, somewhat aloof and haughty. Tanya, the youngest, was mercurial; light on her feet, she always seemed to be running or dancing, and was outgoing, with shining dark eyes. Sonya was of an easier disposition than Lisa, but more sober than Tanya. However, despite a warm smile, she was withdrawn, often melancholy and willful. Tanya wrote that Sonya was "suspicious of happiness, never able to grasp or enjoy it fully." She liked to read, write stories, paint, and play the piano. By age seventeen she had obtained a teacher's certificate.

When Tolstoy decided to court Sonya she was also being wooed by a young soldier named Polivanov in the horse guards. Sonya thought Polivanov would make an acceptable

An 1860 photograph of Sonya Behrs, Tolstoy's future wife (*Courtesy of Mary Evans Picture Library/The Image Works*)

husband, but she was not in love with him. She had loved Tolstoy since she was ten, when he had visited the Behrs on his way to the Caucasus in 1856. She had memorized paragraphs of *Childhood* and kept a copy of the book in a treasured place. She tied a ribbon around the leg of the chair in which Tolstoy sat. During the summer of 1862, while Tolstoy was ostensibly courting her older sister, Sonya had often stared at him with obvious warmth and attention, competing for his attention. The bond between Tolstoy and Sonya was cemented when Lyubov traveled with her three girls to her father's estate, located next to Yasnaya Polyana, in August 1862.

While there, all four had an overnight visit to Yasnaya Polyana and events seemed to conspire to bring Tolstoy and Sonya together. There were not enough beds at Yasnaya Polyana, and Tolstoy improvised one for Sonya using arm chairs covered with linen. The next day, when the entire household and guests went on a picnic, Tolstoy and Sonya rode side by side on horseback while the rest traveled in horse-drawn carriages.

Soon, Tolstoy was in love. He saw in Sonya qualities he had never found in a woman before. He admired her inner quietness and became convinced they shared a deep connection. "How simple and clear you are," he whispered to her while standing on the veranda at Yasnaya Polyana one evening. "How elegant you are," he told her at the dance at her grandfather's estate a few days later.

The evening of the dance, as both Sonya and Tanya recorded in their memoirs years later, the couple found themselves alone after they thought everyone had left the music room. Little did they know, however, that Tanya was hiding under the piano. Tolstoy took a piece of chalk and, on the felt that covered a table top, he wrote the first letters of a series of words, "Y.y.a.y.t.f.h.r.m.c.o.m.a.a.t.i.o.h.f.m" and asked Sonya if she could figure out what it meant. Incredibly, she replied: "Your youth and your thirst for happiness remind me cruelly of my age and the impossibility of happiness for me." He then wrote the first letters of the words of another sentence for her to read out loud: "Your family is mistaken about me and your sister Lisa. Help me to defend myself, you and Tanya." Despite what Sonya and Tanya later wrote, the story seems apocryphal. Perhaps the passage of time turned a less astonishing event into a romantic memory, or it was filtered and exaggerated by Tolstoy's creative imagination—he used the scene in *Anna Karenina* when the character Levin proposes to Kitty.

Unlike Levin, Tolstoy did not propose that night in the music room. Instead, he entered a period of turbulence for both him and Sonya. For Lisa, Sonya's elder sister who had hoped Tolstoy would marry her, it was a time of distress and jealousy. He was inattentive to her and highly sensitive to her sister. When Tolstoy did hand Sonya the letter asking her to be his wife, a letter that had been in his pocket for days as he worked up the courage to give it to her, Lisa flew into a jealous rage and demanded Sonya "refuse right away!" But Lyubov intervened and told Sonya to "Go give him your reply." When Tolstoy took her hands and asked, "Well?" she answered, "Yes, of course!"

Lyubov had to work to get her husband to agree to the marriage. Dr. Behrs thought his eldest daughter should be married first, and that Tolstoy should propose to Lisa. But Lyubov argued that their feelings should be respected and that there were obvious benefits to the match. Tolstoy was a wealthy landowner and an esteemed author. Lisa eventually overcame her resentment and argued for the marriage. Under this pressure, Dr. Behrs capitulated, and the engagement was announced September 17, 1862.

At Tolstoy's insistence, and with Sonya's eager agreement, the wedding was set for the next week. Both families argued for a longer engagement, as was customary, and for time to prepare a trousseau and to plan a grand wedding ceremony. But Tolstoy insisted on a quick wedding and convinced

Although Tolstoy's married life was initially happy, he later realized the concept of marriage and family clashed with his sense of self-sacrifice.

Sonya to forgo a honeymoon and "to begin real life right away, family life," at Yasnaya Polyana.

The long marriage would turn out to be challenging for Tolstoy and Sonya. Although it initially was joyful and seemed to unleash immense creative force in both, it also brought them turbulence and pain that increasingly strained their alliance. They were equal in their energy, passion, and intellect, and both were willing to work hard in pursuit of their artistic and spiritual goals, but both were also capable of casting a dark shadow over the other.

When the newlyweds returned to Yasnaya Polyana, Tolstoy reentered a familiar world. He initially spent his time managing and expanding his estate. He began to keep bees, raise Japanese pigs, plant an apple orchard, grow cabbage on an industrial scale, and to plan the building of a distillery. He was also writing essays on education for *Yasnaya Polyana,* and finishing *The Cossacks.*

Sonya, however, found herself in a life that was entirely new to her. While Tolstoy was seeking meaning and purpose for his life in physical work and writing, Sonya was discovering that the purpose of her life was to be found in terms of her relationship to her husband.

While Tolstoy was sometimes troubled by how significant she had become for him, he needed her love and support too much to have it any other way. Furthermore, he paradoxically came to feel that by marrying he had lost an important part of himself, that marriage, and loving Sonya, were making him "petty and insignificant." It was appalling that his happiness could "depend upon purely material things: a wife, children, health, wealth." He felt that domesticity sometimes caused him to lose his connection to a deeper, more spiritual reality. Soon after Sonya had given birth to Sergey, the first of their thirteen children, he told her he was leaving to join the tsar's army to fight against Polish rebels. When the rebellion was crushed without Russian intervention he suddenly realized how strange his impulse had been: "There was nothing true in it. I am happy with her; but I am dreadfully unhappy with myself. . . . My choice has been made for a long time: letters, art, education and family."

Tolstoy's mood swings did little to diminish Sonya's passionate love for her husband. Increasingly, she came to identify herself through her love for him. Her need for his love and approval often smothered him. She was often jealous, sometimes about his past liaisons that she read about in his diaries, which he had given her to read right before they were married, and sometimes over characters in his stories.

His devotion to the welfare of the peasants also made her jealous. "He makes me sick, with his 'people'! I feel he is going to have to choose between the family, which I personify, and those people he loves so passionately. It's selfish of me? Well, too bad. I live for him and by him and I want it to be the same for him." Tolstoy, too, was torn between his love and commitment to his family and his responsibility to the peasants. The older he got, the stronger the conflict became.

After the birth of Sergey, Tolstoy insisted that Sonya breast-feed the baby, but she was in too much pain. He insisted and said her refusal was just stubbornness and that she had to make a better effort. Despite his fury, she gave the baby to a wet nurse. Tolstoy eventually wrote an apology to her in her diary, but crossed it out soon after when he became angry about something else. This pattern of loving closeness and passionate desire, followed by bitterness and alienation, followed by reconciliation and the return of passion, ran throughout their marriage. Sonya wrote prophetically in her diary during the first year of their marriage: "Little by little I will grow in on myself and poison his existence . . . today I felt that he and I were going each his own way."

This pattern informed a great deal of Tolstoy's fiction. It is the central theme, for example, in the *The Kreutzer Sonata,* published in 1889.

Over the years the strain of this combustible, passionate marriage alienated the couple from one another. But before they became deeply alienated they worked as one. Over their first fifteen years together Sonya was a critical and necessary part of the writing of Tolstoy's two great masterpieces, *War and Peace* and *Anna Karenina.*

seven

Writing the Great Novels

During the first year of marriage, in addition to finishing *The Cossacks,* Tolstoy wrote "Polikushka," a story of peasant life; "Strider," the story of a horse narrated from the horse's point of view; and two chamber plays that were performed by his family. "Polikushka" went largely unnoticed, and he put "Strider" away, unhappy with it, until twenty years later when Sonya asked him to publish it and he revised it.

The Cossacks met a mixed reception when it was published in 1863. A few reviewers, such as the one in *Fatherland Notes,* accused Tolstoy of "romantic[izing] drunkenness, piracy, theft, and blood-lust," and making his main character, Olenin, "the representative of civilized society . . . debased, degraded, defeated."

An Ilya Yefimovich Repin painting of Russian Cossacks. Tolstoy romanticized the lives of these gypsylike people in his novel *The Cossacks.*

Other reviewers had a more temperate but mixed response. They generally admired the way Tolstoy had caught and conveyed "the very breadth of the Caucasus," or, as Turgenev wrote, "the contrast between civilization and primitive, unspoiled nature." The poet Fet wrote to Tolstoy that "*The Cossacks* is a sort of masterpiece," which showed "the ineffable superiority of [Tolstoy's] talent."

During the composition of *The Cossacks,* Tolstoy matured into the masterful novelist who, over the next decade and a half, would write *War and Peace* and *Anna Karenina.* He knew he was reaching the pinnacle of his talent and skill. "I have never felt my mental and even moral powers so free and ready for work," he wrote to his cousin, Alexandra Tolstoy, on October 17, 1863.

The first of the huge masterpieces to be written was *War and Peace.* Tolstoy spent more than six years writing

An artist's rendition of Tolstoy's Anna Karenina on a Russian postcard
(Courtesy of Lebrecht Music & Arts/The Image Works)

it. Members of his family, friends and acquaintances, the events that occurred in his life over those six years, as well as the places he had seen and houses he and his family had lived in, were all incorporated into his epic fiction. Tanya, Sonya's younger sister, was the model for Natasha Rostov, one of the most charming characters in the book. Tolstoy studied the way Tanya moved, what brought her happiness, as well as what brought her sadness, to build the character of Natasha. He spent so much time with Tanya during the writing of *War and Peace* and was so attentive to her that Sonya became jealous.

While Tolstoy concentrated on his work, Sonya managed Yasnaya Polyana. She was not merely responsible for the typical domestic duties of a wife; she oversaw the management of the vast estate.

Sonya took on these extra duties while also working—often until the early hours of the morning—as her husband's secretary. Over the six years she hand-copied the manuscript of *War and Peace* seven times. This work entailed deciphering Tolstoy's crabbed, almost illegible handwriting, recopying sections to insert his revisions and to take out his deletions. She even inserted his corrections on the publisher's galleys after her handwritten pages had been set in print, and then yet again after he had revised her insertions. Sonya also acted as the first reader and, while she offered criticisms and no doubt helped him to make improvements, her awe at the magnitude and greatness of *War and Peace* never wavered.

Tolstoy worked with great concentration. He possessed vigorous intellectual energy and great physical strength, as well as a penetrating and subtle genius for observation and introspection. His principal fault had always been his divided nature and inability to remain dedicated to any single idea or project. Now it seemed that the stability of his marriage and the devotion and commitment of his wife provided the emotional security he needed to focus on this six-year project.

Psychologically, Tolstoy was motivated by his fear of death and desire for immortality. He wanted to be remembered and loved when he was gone. Later in life, after the fear of death had almost destroyed him, he managed to overcome it to some extent by immersing himself in his own form of Christianity.

But in 1863 he strove with all his might to obtain immortality and, although it ultimately left him emotionally and spiritually unsatisfied, the novel he produced attained it.

War and Peace grew out of an earlier unfinished work, *The Decembrists*, which was based on an historical event. In December 1825, a group of Russian army officers, unhappy with the accession of Nicholas I to the throne, attempted a coup. The officers were arrested and exiled to Siberia. However, as Tolstoy worked on *The Decembrists*, he found it necessary to delve deeper into the past to explain the motivations of the plotters. In the process, he realized the story of Russia's long struggle against the French armies of Napoleon Bonaparte was the story he really wanted to tell. He set the beginning of the novel that would eventually be titled *War and Peace* in 1805.

In *War and Peace,* Tolstoy brings the events of the years from 1805 to 1812 to life through the experiences and observations of a multitude of characters drawn from Russian nobility. From the drawing rooms to the battlefields, the characters participate in, and come to terms with, the long, perilous war. Tolstoy also works in the societal and philosophical changes propelled by the war. Much of the novel's power is in the magnitude of its scope, juxtaposed with the minuteness of the carefully selected details Tolstoy uses to bring his scenes to life.

Underlying the narrative is Tolstoy's deterministic view of history. In a long epilogue he explicitly sets out his theory that individuals, regardless of their stature, have little effect on the progress of history. According to Tolstoy, Napoleon was no more critical to the war historians have named after him than was the lowest soldier in his army. That Napoleon thinks he is directing history, when in reality he is being swept along by the historical tide that carries us all, is vanity.

The more overtly religious themes that came to dominate Tolstoy's later work were not yet formed into a cohesive philosophy in *War and Peace*. They begin to emerge in the sections of *Anna Karenina* devoted to Levin's, one of the major characters, Christian awakening and growing social consciousness. At this stage Tolstoy was not concerned with social messages. He still believed in the power of art. "The aims of art," he wrote in July 1865:

> [Are] incommensurable . . . with the aims of socialism. An artist's mission must not be to produce an irrefutable solution to a problem, but to compel us to love life in all its countless and inexhaustible manifestations. If I were told I might write a book in which I should demonstrate beyond any doubt the correctness of my opinions on every social problem, I should not waste two hours at it; but if I were told that what I wrote would be read twenty years from now by people who are children today, and that they would weep and laugh over my book and love life more because of it, then I should devote all my life and strength to such a work.

Later, in a work entitled *What Is Art?*, Tolstoy would recant an "art for art's sake" aesthetic and renounce his earlier fiction because it "infected" readers with vain emotions and imaginary pleasures. He wanted to replace it with work that would transform the human soul by flooding it with a sense of what is good and how life had to be lived.

War and Peace was published in 1869 in a six volume edition. Although readers were slow to warm to the earlier sections when they had been published serially, response to the publication of the entire massive work was overwhelmingly positive.

Despite the book's success, Tolstoy was wracked with

deep despair and a breakdown of physical health when the work was completed. He "engaged in long and laborious meditations," Sonya wrote in her diary in 1870. "Often he said his brain hurt him, some painful process was going on inside it, everything was over for him, it was time to die." In writing *War and Peace,* he had lived with the deaths of his fictional characters so long that they had come to seem more real than many of the people around him. Now it was time to turn back to the disappointments of the real world.

Tolstoy had taken time out from working on *War and Peace* to defend, before a military tribunal, a half-mad peasant soldier who had struck a superior officer in a fit of what Tolstoy considered to be justifiable rage. He was not able to save the man from the firing squad. His diary reveals he was still thinking about universal injustice. He had taken note of revolutionary and writer Proudhon's dictum that "property is theft" and had come to think it was true. Nevertheless, he continued to live in a world of privileges. This conflict between his beliefs and his life tormented him and helped to convince him further of the meaninglessness of life.

On a trip to see some land he was thinking of buying, some five hundred miles from Yasnaya Polyana, Tolstoy was suddenly overcome with the terror of death. He had stopped for the night at an inn when, "My whole being ached with the need to live, the right to live, and, at the same moment, I felt death at work. And it was awful, being torn apart inside." Shaken by this experience, when he was convinced that he was in the presence of death, Tolstoy immediately returned to Yasnaya Polyana.

Without his all-consuming work on *War and Peace* to

occupy his energies for the next three years, from 1870 until March 18, 1873—the day he began to write *Anna Karenina*— he slept, played bezique, skied, skated, and exercised. He also read deeply in Shakespeare, the German writer Goethe, the French writer Molière, and the Russian masters Pushkin and Gogol. When he began reading the works of the philosopher Schopenhauer, he became fascinated by his philosophy, which emphasized the futility of desire and said that salvation came from asceticism and service to others.

Despite his almost constant self-reproaches at his laziness, Tolstoy was quite active during this period. During the spring of 1870 he portrayed himself in a letter to a friend as "covered with sweat and carrying my ax and spade . . . a thousand miles from any thought of art." That summer he described himself, "thanks be to God . . . as stupid as a horse."

Then, in autumn, Sonya wrote in her diary: "Leo sits behind a stack of books, portraits and pictures, frowning and reading, examining, taking notes. In the evening, when the children are in bed, he tells me his plans and what he wants to write. He has chosen the period of Peter the Great . . . I think he is going to write another epic like *War and Peace*."

Tolstoy was uncertain about his plans. "I am in a most exasperating state of mind, with wild schemes, doubts of myself and hard mental labor all intermingled. Perhaps this is the prelude to a period of happy and confident work, and perhaps, on the contrary, I shall never write another word."

Tolstoy was researching a novel about Peter the Great, the tsar during the sixteenth and early seventeenth century who had tried to modernize Russia. Tolstoy started and stopped several times, but the project never came to life. One reason for this failure was that the more research he did the more he became disgusted with his subject, who he decided was no more a "great man" than Napoleon, whom he had disparaged in *War and Peace*. In the earlier novel he had put forth his theory

Peter the Great

that history moved at its own inexorable pace. To turn now to a novel about a "great man" contradicted this view. He stopped working on the novel and began to ponder something much different—a story about the Russian aristocracy set in current times. This would allow him to develop his ideas about many of the moral concerns that preoccupied him in his own life.

All Sonya could see was his failure to get started on a project, which she thought was the one thing that could make him reasonably happy and content. In December 1870 she wrote: "His lack of direction is a great trial to him. He is ashamed of it. . . . Sometimes he thinks he is losing his mind." Instead of writing, he studied Greek, which he enjoyed and mastered quickly.

After giving birth to a daughter on February 12, 1871, Sonya contracted puerperal fever, a painful, life-threatening infection of the urinary tract. Tolstoy was terrified that she was going to die. After she recovered, his anxiety focused on himself. "I have never been so depressed in all my life. I have lost the joy of living," he wrote to a friend. He had also lost interest in his wife: "Something in us has broken."

Sonya joined him in despair: "I have lost my faith in happiness and life." Desperate to do something, she persuaded Tolstoy to try the kumys cure that had done him some good the summer before their marriage. However, even in Samara, among his old Bashkir friends who remembered him from nine years before, Tolstoy experienced "a physical feeling of dread," as if "the soul becomes separated from the body."

However, when he returned to Yasnaya Polyana in early August 1871, Tolstoy's health had improved and his spirits had revived. He bought some land, which also lifted his spirits, but before long he was again overwhelmed by depression and fears that his life was over. He lost interest in everything; nothing gave him pleasure; there was nothing he wanted.

When N. N. Strakhov, a literary critic, philosopher, editor of several important Russian periodicals, as well as the first biographer of Dostoevsky, Tolstoy's chief rival as Russia's most revered novelist, visited Yasnaya Polyana that autumn, Tolstoy's spirits rebounded. He was strengthened by the tonic of Strakhov's praise.

His spirits buoyed by Strakhov's company, Tolstoy began to work on his *Readers* or *ABC Books* for schoolchildren.

The *Readers* ended up being more than seven hundred pages long and were filled with instructive anecdotes and moral folk tales, translations of great literature, and sections on mathematics and the sciences.

Tolstoy also reopened his school, but the bureaucrats in charge of schools gave Tolstoy's educational endeavors no support. In addition, the first reviewers objected to his *Readers,* calling them attacks on conventional models and methods of education—which they were, as he had intended. Tolstoy published an open letter to the chairman of the Moscow-based Society for the Education of the People, asserting that "freedom is the sole criterion in pedagogy," and that with his *Readers* he hoped to "give pupils for the smallest price, the greatest quantity of comprehensible material."

Sonya thought the school books were a waste of Tolstoy's time and energy. Publishers were offering him generous contracts to write another book. "It isn't so much the money," Sonya wrote to her sister, "I love his literary works, I admire them and they move me. . . . I despise this *Reader,* this arithmetic, this grammar, and I cannot pretend to be interested in them."

Adding to her distress, Sonya was pregnant again. Instead of being with child, she wanted "gaiety, idle chatter, elegance. I would like to be liked, to hear people tell me I am beautiful, and I would like Leo to see and hear them too. He ought to abandon the isolation—sometimes he wearies of it—and live with me the way ordinary mortals do." Gradually, their different temperaments began to undermine their love and happiness.

Finally, in March 1873, Sonya was able to report happily that Tolstoy was again working hard on a long project.

Tolstoy writing at his desk. *(Courtesy of Lebrecht Music & Arts/The Image Works)*

Although time would reveal that, unlike when he was writing *War and Peace*, the new book did not consume him, she was overjoyed to see him putting his momentous talent to work.

The story of an unfaithful society wife and the tragedy that ensues from her adultery had been incubating for years. Then in January 1872, a local woman, Anna Pirogova, who had lived with a man for years before he had decided to marry someone else, threw herself under a train. Suddenly, Tolstoy had the terrible climactic scene for the new novel. He even went to the train station to see the body and watch as the autopsy was performed.

When he started writing his new novel Tolstoy thought he was back to his old self. In May 1873 he wrote to Strakhov: "I am writing a novel that has nothing to do with Peter the Great. . . . This is my first real novel and I am taking it very much to heart. I am completely wrapped up in it."

Anna Karenina is structured in two parallel narratives, both about love and passion. The narrative involving the title character is about adultery and its tragic consequences. When the reader first meets Anna she is married to a man twenty years her senior. While he is content with his life and his job as a government official, Anna is bored and terrified that her life is passing by while she is trapped in such a mundane existence. When she meets an army officer, Count Vronsky, who is as exciting and fun-loving as her husband is dull, she falls passionately in love and begins an affair. After confessing the affair to her husband and recovering from a life-threatening illness, she leaves the country with Vronsky. However, over the course of her relationship she becomes increasingly upset as she realizes he is losing interest in her. Finally, she slips into a tormented depression and commits suicide by throwing herself under a train.

Contrasted to this tragic tale of illicit love is the relationship of Levin and Kitty. Initially, Kitty has eyes only for Count Vronsky, but when she loses him to Anna, she turns her attention to Levin, who has pined for Kitty for months. Although she had been drawn to the glamorous Vronsky, Kitty soon comes to love and respect the quietly honorable Levin. During the course of the novel their love grows deep, although it is never as passionate as Anna and Vronsky's affair. They marry and move to Levin's estate, where they begin a life very similar to the one Tolstoy and Sonya lived at Yasnaya Polyana.

By juxtaposing the narratives, Tolstoy is able to give life to his conviction that the love that develops between Kitty and Levin is superior to the passion that sweeps Anna off her feet and eventually leads to her suicide. However, Tolstoy was careful to not present stock characters to make his moral points. He refuses to give Kitty and Levin all the "good" traits and Anna, or even Vronsky, all the "bad" traits. Anna is probably the most intriguing character in the novel, although she makes choices the author finds abhorrent. Early in the novel Tolstoy is clearly sympathetic with Anna's fear that her life is passing her by; it is her decision to escape her suffocating existence by running off with Vronsky that dooms her. Levin, the character most like Tolstoy himself, experiences many of the same spiritual crises that Tolstoy did. He is sometimes foolish and prone to enthusiasms he is unable to sustain over the long term. As in *War and Peace*, Tolstoy takes care to develop complex and complicated characters.

The writing of *Anna Karenina* did not bring Tolstoy the peace and contentment he sought, however. Even while still writing, and despite the public reception to its serial publication, which was "nothing less than delirium" in Strakhov's phrase, Tolstoy was becoming estranged from the book. In a reply to Strakhov's letter reporting on the book's success he wrote about other activities: "I am directing the seventy schools that have opened in our district. . . . I am continuing . . . educational research . . . teaching my older children myself . . . correcting proofs of the second *Reader.*" While praise of *Anna Karenina* was "music to my ears . . . I am sure there never has been a writer more indifferent to success than I am . . . if it is success." Later he wrote to his cousin Alexandra, "I'm sick and tired of my Anna K." In another note to Strakhov he complained, "Ah, if only somebody else could finish *Anna Karenina* for me."

As his disenchantment grew, Tolstoy began to minimize his achievement. He wrote to his son Ilya: "What's so difficult about describing how an officer gets entangled with a woman? There's nothing difficult in that, and above all, nothing worthwhile. It's bad, and it serves no purpose."

Tolstoy also used the book, primarily through the character of Levin, to discourse about social and political issues, including the hot topics of pacifism and nationalism. Partly, this was motivated by current events.

In April 1877, Russia entered a war that had broken out between the Ottoman Turks and the Serbs and Montenegrins, who had rebelled against Turkish control. When Russia declared war against Turkey, volunteers rushed to fight in support of their fellow Slavs. When Tolstoy used the character of Levin to criticize the war and Russian nationalism, Katkov, editor of the *Russian Herald,* which was scheduled to publish the last installment of his novel, now refused to issue it.

Levin's pacifism reflects a deeper change in Tolstoy's thought, which is suggested by the concluding sentence of *Anna Karenina*: "'[F]rom now on my life,' Levin thinks, 'no matter what happens to me . . . is not only not meaningless as it was before, but it has the incontestable meaning of the goodness I have the power to put into it!'" Tolstoy's own life was turning from art toward a quest to know "good" and then to live in accordance with it. This would eventually move him to renounce his former life, including his class privilege and artistic aspirations.

By the time he finished *Anna Karenina,* Tolstoy was in a spiritual crisis. In the novel, Levin thinks "he was horrified not so much by death as by a life without the slightest knowledge of where it came from, what it was for." Tolstoy was more convinced than ever that his life and the lives of all men of his privileged class were wasted in materialism and vanity. Many were turning to what he saw as the new faith of science, but science held out only material knowledge—not wisdom. The only solution to his despair was to commit to an unquestioning faith in God.

Tolstoy's vision of God was not intellectual, however. God could only be known by the experience of His presence. Tolstoy saw himself as a man who had once had powerful wings, but he had broken them by indulging the desires of his body and his personal ambition. Now he was determined to repair the damage.

eight

Rebirth

Tolstoy's discontent with his life, his terror of death, and Sonya's distress at the course he was taking, began to define their marriage during the early 1870s. As a man who had been controlled by passions he was determined to master, Tolstoy wanted to free his soul, the pure eternal part of himself, from what he considered to be the sinful and mortal part of himself. The only way to defeat death was to break the self-centered attachment he had to his physical being. This attachment gained its strength through his lust for things and sensations, and he was determined to break the cycle of desire and despair. The more practical Sonya, however, clung to the material world. As long as her husband and her children and grandchildren were alive, she wanted them to have a good life, and for this they needed food, shelter, education, clothing, and social connections. She was not ready to give up excitement and worldly pleasures; Tolstoy wanted to transcend desire, to need and to want nothing.

Sonya wrote in her diary in 1881:

> Until about 1877 L[eo] N[ikolaievich]'s religious feelings were vague. . . . He was never an outright unbeliever, nor was he a very committed believer. This caused L.N. terrible torments. . . . [F]rom close contact with . . . the holy wanderers and pilgrims, he was deeply impressed by their lucid, unshakable faith, and terrified by his own lack of it. . . . [S]uddenly he resolved wholeheartedly to follow the same path. . . . He started going to church, keeping the fasts, saying his prayers, and observing the laws of the Church. . . . [L]ittle by little L.N. saw to his horror what a discrepancy there was between Christianity and the Church . . . that the Church, hand in hand with the Government, had conspired against Christianity. . . . [Consequently,] he has begun to study, translate, and interpret the Gospels. . . . His soul is now happy, he says. He has seen the light . . . and this light has illuminated his whole view of the world. . . . He now has millions of men as his brothers. Before, his wealth and his estate were his own—now if a poor man asks for something he must have it. . . . He does not appear to be as happy as I should wish, and has become quiet, meditative, and taciturn. We almost never see those cheerful exuberant moods of his now, which used to enchant us all so much. . . . [H]e suffers deeply for all the human misery and poverty he sees about him . . . for all the hatred, injustice, and oppression in the world.

Although their marriage became tormented during their later years together, Sonya always understood her husband, even if she did not share his convictions. But they were at odds. She longed for his love and companionship and to enjoy with him the rewards of the fame and wealth he had worked so hard to attain. He, on the other hand, wished for nothing but to give

Tolstoy felt the Russian Orthodox Church perverted the teaching of Christ, and he distanced himself from the church soon after his recommitment to Christianity. *(Library of Congress)*

away everything he owned, denounce his past literary work, and renounce his fame.

Tolstoy broke with the state-sanctioned Russian Orthodox Church two years after he recommitted himself to Christianity. It became impossible for him to ignore his belief, expressed earlier in a scene in *War and Peace,* that the Orthodox Church perverted Christ's teaching.

Tolstoy wrote four theological works in the early 1880s that set forth his belief that "the foundation of [Christ's] teaching is that to achieve salvation it is necessary, every day and every hour of every day, to think of God, of one's soul, and therefore to set the love of one's neighbor above mere bestial existence." Religion was not about rituals and abstract beliefs, he said. It was about absolute love for every living thing, not abstractly and intellectually, but through personal experience and conviction. *The Kingdom of God Is Within*

You is the title of one of his books about his theology. On his deathbed, Tolstoy dictated to his daughter, Alexandra, the sentence, "God is not love, but the more [love] there is in man, the more is God made manifest in him, and the more truly does he exist."

Tolstoy, who had always condemned authoritarianism and coercion, opposed both the church and the Russian government. "Religion, as long as it is religion," he wrote, "cannot by its very essence, be subject to authority (war, torture, plunder, theft, everything bound up with government). That is why a government must make certain of its control over religion." The Christian love Tolstoy embraced preached nonviolence and responding to evil with good instead of resisting it.

When Tsar Alexander II was assassinated by members of a revolutionary group called "People's Will" on March 2, 1881, Tolstoy was horrified. Alexander had been a liberal leader. He had finally freed the serfs, ended the Crimean War, granted amnesty to the exiled Decembrists who had risen up

This painting shows the coronation of Tsar Alexander III.

against his father in 1825, and he was planning to introduce a Russian constitution. Although he supported these policies, Tolstoy remained opposed to the State on theological grounds and the tsar's liberalism was not enough to satisfy his vision of a better world. But revolutionary violence violated the core values of Christian love and nonresistance to evil to which he was dedicated.

Distressed as he was by the assassination, Tolstoy was even more troubled by the execution of the assassins that would follow. Punishment of any sort violated the teachings of the Gospel, he said. More practically, he was convinced that executing the tsar's assassins would continue a cycle of violence that would culminate, as it did some forty years later, in a blood-drenched revolution. In hopes of diverting the executions, Tolstoy wrote a letter to the new tsar, Alexander III, imploring him to forgive his father's assassins.

Tolstoy sent the letter to Strakhov on March 17, 1881, and asked him to present it to the tsar's Minister to the Holy Synod, the governing body of the Russian Orthodox Church, Konstantin Pobyedonostsev. He hoped Pobyedonostsev would give the letter to Alexander, but Pobyedonostsev refused. "[Y]our faith ha[s] nothing in common with mine," he wrote to Tolstoy. "[M]y Christ [i]s not your Christ. My Christ is a man of strength and truth who heals the weak, and yours seemed to me to be a weak man himself in need of healing." Tolstoy had made an enemy of the most powerful man in Russia.

Sonya was worried when Tolstoy became an open opponent of the government and was distressed by the changes his religious beliefs made in his personality. "I often have little quarrels with Leo now. . . . It must be because we have

As Tolstoy's humanitarian efforts increased, he began to befriend Russian prisoners and write about their misery. *(Library of Congress)*

begun to live as Christians. . . . he has grown pale, his health is poor and he is more subdued and somber than before."

As Tolstoy turned his energy to the sad matters of human misery he became less playful and tolerant with his family. He visited prisoners, went to court with them, stood on the railway platform when they were deported to Siberia, and wrote about their wretchedness. He spoke for those who could not describe their suffering themselves. As he established deeper bonds with outcasts he came to resent the bond he had with his family. "The family is flesh," he wrote. "Abandon the family. . . . The family is only a body. . . . live not for the family but for God."

When Tolstoy, dressed like a peasant, set out on foot, on June 10, 1881, for the monastery at Optina-Pustyn, it was an attempt to transform himself into one of the thousands of Russians who trekked across the country and renounced all worldliness. He wanted to find the part of himself uncorrupted by civilization. "One cannot imagine how new, important, and useful it is to the soul," he wrote to Sonya during his trek, "to see how God's world lives, the true world, the great world, not the one we have arranged for ourselves and never stepped outside of."

But Tolstoy only escaped so far from his arranged world. Servants followed behind on the road carrying clean linen and money used to buy Tolstoy heavy socks when his peasant footwear made blisters on his feet. When they arrived at the monastery, they were mistaken for beggars and not permitted to eat in the pilgrims' refectory. They were forced to sit at a long table with the other wretches and given "borscht, kasha, kvass. One cup for four people," Tolstoy noted. "Everything is good. They eat hungrily." Afterwards, at the entrance to the filthy third-class dormitory where bug-infested straw pallets covered the floor, Tolstoy threw up his "good" dinner, and one of his servants, also dressed like a peasant, slipped a ruble to one of the attending monks and secured a small room in which someone was already sleeping. He made up a bed for Tolstoy with the clean sheets he had carried with him.

In the morning the rumor had spread through the monastery that Count Tolstoy was visiting. Tolstoy was moved immediately to the monastery's best room where he changed his clothes, put on his boots, and asked if he might have an audience with Father Ambrose, a celebrated hermit who resided at the monastery and whom pilgrims waited, sometimes for days, to see to ask for advice. Tolstoy was admitted immediately, and the two spent four hours in conversation. Ambrose tried to bring Tolstoy back to the Orthodox Church—without success.

Tolstoy's return to Yasnaya Polyana began on foot, but after a little way, he took a third-class railroad train and conversed with the peasants. He had wired ahead the time of his return and when he arrived at the station he was met by his coachman and driven back to Yasnaya Polyana in a carriage pulled by a pair of horses.

Tolstoy was sensitive to the charge of hypocrisy brought against him by his opponents and to the reproaches of his adherents who lived his teachings more fully than he did. He laid the blame for his failure on his inability to break from his family.

> I have unceasingly prepared myself to bear the cross I know: prison and the gallows; now I see before me a completely different cross, I am placed against my will in the position of a spiritual weakling and by my way of life I am compelled to destroy the very things I live for. . . . I am unable to tear myself free from these awful cobwebs in which I have become entangled. . . . [M]y conscience will not let me.

When Sonya insisted they move to Moscow in September 1881 because the children were coming to the age when schools and society were necessary, Tolstoy was disgusted once again by the luxury in which the upper class lived—and which defined his own household. He volunteered to be a census taker in the worst neighborhoods of Moscow for the 1882 census and came into direct contact with the plight of the poor. He was heartsick. He wrote *The Moscow Census*, decrying the wretchedness he had seen and calling not for charity but for Christian change in each person's heart.

Writing became a social action for Tolstoy. In *War and Peace*, he had scoffed at the idea that writers could influence history, but after his conversion, he took it as his duty to try to change hearts with his pen.

In response to calls for help in raising money for the people living in famine-stricken areas of Russia in the summer of 1891, he first responded that "The most effective remedy against the famine is to write something which might touch the hearts of the rich." He had already written that charity was simply the way the rich gave back to the poor a little of what they had stolen from them in the accumulation of their wealth—an easy way to assuage their conscience. But in September he traveled with his daughters Tanya and Masha to Pirogovo, and the plight of the starvation was so bad he decided that it was necessary to take immediate action, despite his opposition to charity as an easy way out for the wealthy. He convinced Sonya to allot some of their money, which she controlled, for a relief project. In the blighted region, Tolstoy, Tanya, and Masha bought firewood and organized kitchens and bakeries.

At first Sonya had thought that Tolstoy was impelled by vanity and the need to prove his unselfishness to his critics, but the work he devoted to the relief efforts convinced her he was serious. On November 3, 1891, the *Russian News* published a letter she wrote to the editor reporting on the famine, her family's efforts to help, and soliciting contributions.

The letter appeared in every Russian paper and was reprinted in translations throughout Europe and the United States. Within two weeks Sonya had collected more than 13,000 rubles and was overseeing shipments of food, clothing, and medicine to the relief workers. "There is a great deal to be said against all this," Tolstoy wrote to his friend, the painter Nicholas Gay. "There is the problem of the relations between those who eat and those who give food. . . . But it would be impossible for me to stay home and write." Working together on famine relief brought Tolstoy and Sonya close to each other for the time being. "Every night I see you in my dreams," he wrote to her.

Tolstoy's active role in famine relief did not, however, endear him to the ruling circles of Russia, especially when it was accompanied by arguments

This Russian poster is captioned, "Remember Those Who Starve!" Tolstoy organized a relief project for starving peasants during the famine of 1891.

such as the ones in an essay entitled "Help for the Hungry": "The people are starving because we eat too much. This has always been true. . . . The privileged classes must go to the people with the attitude that they are guilty."

This conflicted directly with the official government line, which denied that the famine even existed. Tsar Alexander III was convinced his father had made a mistake by trying to liberalize Russian society and government. A resurgence of authoritarianism characterized his rein. Government propaganda began portraying Tolstoy as a devil who had rejected the only true Church. People were actually encouraged to starve rather than go to the kitchens he had set up, because the devil was supplying Tolstoy with the food and anyone who accepted his aid was endangering his eternal soul. A tsarist newspaper characterized Tolstoy's writing as "the most rabid, wild-eyed form of socialism in comparison to which the pamphlets of the clandestine agitators are milk and honey. . . . He openly preaches social revolution. . . .he affirms that the rich subsist on the sweat of the people, consuming everything they possess and produce." One doesn't have to sympathize with the callousness and authoritarianism of the writer to realize that he understood exactly what Tolstoy was saying.

Minister Pobyedonostsev did his part in the vilification of Tolstoy. After the tsar had been moved by a reading he heard in January 1887 of Tolstoy's play *The Power of Darkness*, Pobyedonostsev reminded him that the play was a "negation of the ideal," caused a "degradation of the moral sense," was "an offense to good taste," and that "the play cannot be performed. . . . This ignominious L. Tolstoy must be stopped. He is nothing but a nihilist and a non-believer." Staging of the play was accordingly forbidden.

Tolstoy was not intimidated. "I write what I think," he wrote to a worried Sonya in 1892.

> [T]hings that could not possibly be acceptable to the government and upper classes—and have been doing so for the last twelve years; I do not write that way by accident, but on purpose, and not only do I have no intention of justifying myself, but I trust those who believe I should, will, if not justify their own conduct, then at least clear themselves of the crimes they have committed.

The problem was that the people Tolstoy thought were criminals did not agree. They did not think they had done anything wrong and had no guilt. They did, however, believe that Tolstoy was dangerous, but they were stymied in their desire to quiet him because his novels had made him world famous. He had to be dealt with carefully. The tsar told his minister of the interior: "I will ask you not to touch Tolstoy. I have no desire to make a martyr of him and provoke a general uprising." Unfortunately, Tolstoy's disciples were not so immunized. In his last years, Tolstoy was tormented that many of those who lived by his teachings were punished while he was left unscathed. Repeatedly, but to no avail, he called upon the authorities to imprison him instead of them.

In 1887, Alexander extended military conscription to the Dukhobors, a Russian Christian sect. The Dukhobors lived as farmers and believed in a faith similar to Tolstoy's. They practiced pacifism, vegetarianism, abstinence from tobacco and alcohol, and governing themselves according to democratic and egalitarian principles. They resisted the tsar's order, even going so far as to destroy all their weapons in 1894. Tolstoy came to their defense with a broadside that was banned in Russia but printed in the *London Times* called, "The Persecution of Christians in Russia in 1895."

In order to raise money to support the Dukhobors he even resumed work on a novel he had begun in 1889. He wanted to write a commercially successful work like the two great novels he had repudiated. It took a while to complete, but when he published *Resurrection* at the turn of the century he gave all the proceeds to the Dukhobors, which enabled them to leave Russia and settle in Canada.

Although formally it might resemble his past work, thematically *Resurrection* reflected his new consciousness. It is a story about a young peasant woman, Maslova, who is seduced and abandoned by a young man of the aristocracy, much like the real-life story of Tolstoy and Aksinya Bazykin. Maslova becomes a prostitute and is arrested and brought to trial. One of the jurors, Nekhlyudov, is the man who is responsible for her fall. After she is sent to prison he abandons his life of privilege and follows her to Siberia. Before he would allow it to be published in Russia the censor expunged nearly five hundred passages from *Resurrection*. As with most of his work written during the last decades of his life, the full text of *Resurrection* appeared first in an English translation of an original text that was smuggled out of Russia.

Tolstoy *(front)* with his friend and disciple, V. G. Chertkov

In the summer of 1883, Gabriel Rusanov, a young man who had been moved by Tolstoy's *Confession,* visited him at Yasnaya Polyana. As they spoke of the ideas that had changed Rusanov's life, he told Tolstoy the story of V. G. Chertkov. At twenty-seven, Chertkov, the son of a wealthy adjutant general, who moved in the highest circles of St. Petersburg society and was a captain of the Guards, resigned from the army and gave up the debauched life he had been leading. He began to study the Gospels and actively follow the teachings of Christ. Retiring to his large estate, he devoted himself and his wealth to projects to better the life of the peasantry. He endeavored to give up every luxury and to live as simply and frugally as he could.

Tolstoy sensed that Chertkov was a man who embodied his own ideals. When they met in October 1883 they formed a fast bond. Their meeting marked the direction Tolstoy's life was to take until his death. Together they started the Intermediary Press in order to print and distribute Tolstoy's new Christian anarchist writings.

Chertkov also began to supplant Sonya in Tolstoy's life. No longer was she the confidante who was the first to see his writings. Moreover, the influence of the disciple, whose thinking lacked the subtlety of Tolstoy's, began to dominate the older master. Sincere belief in his own righteousness, Chertkov sharpened the conflict between Tolstoy and his wife. Sonya wished her husband to retain his copyrights, to keep his estate, and to devote himself to writing books such as *War and Peace* and *Anna Karenina*. Chertkov wanted Tolstoy to follow his own teaching more rigorously—to leave his home and privileges, renounce his land and copyrights, and write the radical Christian-anarchist tracts that Sonya considered a waste of his talents.

Tormented as Tolstoy slipped away, Sonya began suffering fits and rages against her husband, his disciple, and herself, which increased in ferocity and apparent irrationality as Tolstoy continued to draw ever closer to Chertkov.

Sonya expressed her point of view in 1891, as she was copying Tolstoy's essay, "On Life," and translating it into French: "When I was young . . . before my marriage, I aspired to the good described in it with all my heart and soul, the fruit of self-denial and the gift of oneself to others. I aspired to the ascetic life. But fate gave me a family and now I live for that."

Not surprisingly, Tolstoy's Christian philosophy influenced the way he thought about sex, which had caused him so much turmoil and conflict throughout his life. Before, he had seen marriage as the solution to the problem of lust. By the late 1880s, when he was beginning his seventh decade, he began to see marriage as an institution that promoted and legitimatized the sin of lust. "The goal of our life should be," he wrote to his son Ilya at the time he was about to be married, "not to find joy in marriage, but to bring more love and truth into the world. . . . The most selfish and hateful life of all is that of two beings who unite in order to enjoy life."

According to Sonya's diary, this new position on sex in marriage was not merely an older man's position, one taken when the drive for sexual gratification no longer pressed so insistently. She recorded that even during this period her husband was sometimes overwhelmed by sexual desire and continued to have sexual relations with his wife. Obviously his struggle with sexual desire predated his religious conversion. During the last years of his life he became convinced passion brought out an animalistic need to possess another person completely, that sexual impulse was at the core of the impulse to be a master and owner. Passion inevitably turns the desired into property.

In *The Kreutzer Sonata,* a novella recounting the story of Pozdnyshev, a man who murders his wife when he is caught in the snares of violent jealousy, Tolstoy expresses the revulsion he had come to feel toward marriage. The story of how he came to despise and murder his wife is told by Pozdnyshev during a train journey. Pozdnyshev gives a full explanation of Tolstoy's views. *The Kreutzer Sonata* describes a marriage very much like Tolstoy's and Sonya's. If read as a tract, the moral conforms to these words Tolstoy wrote Chertkov in November 1888:

> Let everyone try not to marry and, if he be married, to live with his wife as brother and sister. . . . [T]his will mean the end of the human race? . . . What a great misfortune! The antediluvian animals are gone from the earth, the human animal will disappear too. . . . I have no more pity for these two-footed beasts than for the ichthyosaurus.

Sonya knew that Tolstoy was describing their tempestuous relationship and his wildly ambivalent nature in *The Kreutzer Sonata,* and that the novella would be read as a *roman a clef* with details about their private relationship. To make matters worse, she was pregnant with their last child. He preaches abstinence, she imagined scornful critics mocking, and continues relations with his wife.

When the censor prohibited publication of *The Kreutzer Sonata* on grounds of immorality, Sonya sought and obtained an audience with the tsar and obtained permission from him to publish *The Kreutzer Sonata* in Volume XIII of Tolstoy's *Complete Works.* Tolstoy had given over his copyrights to her, and Sonya had set up her own publishing venture—after conferring with Dostoevsky's widow, who had done the same for her husband's work.

Not being able to publish *The Kreutzer Sonata* would have meant a substantial financial loss, but even more was at stake. "I wanted to show myself in public so they could see how little I resemble a victim," Sonya wrote in her diary. "If the book had been inspired by me," she reasoned, "if it did portray my relations with Leo Nikolayevich, I should certainly have done nothing to further its circulation, anyone who thinks for a moment will realize that." She added, "The emperor said I was simple, sincere and engaging; he had not supposed I was still so young and good-looking. All this is highly flattering to my woman's vanity." She clearly still longed for the excitement of social gatherings, sparkling friendships, and intoxicating flirtations, all the things that Tolstoy detested.

Music was another of the pleasures of life that Tolstoy struggled to renounce. He had always been deeply affected by music and had spent many hours himself at the piano, which he played well. In *The Kreutzer Sonata,* he reveals the sensual power music exerted over him.

Sonya's own love of music led her into a passionate friendship with the composer and pianist Sergey Tanayev. Although their relationship was probably never consummated, she came to have deep feelings for the composer. Tanayev stayed with the Tolstoys over the summer in 1895 and 1896, and he often visited them during the year when they were in Moscow. At this time Sonya was lonely and vulnerable and in need of an emotionally compelling attachment. Apart from the brutal vicissitudes of her relationship with her husband, she was tormented by the death of her last and beloved child, Vanechka, in 1895. Tolstoy, although deeply pained by the loss, had made his peace with death as being God's will. Sonya was not able to subsume her grief so quickly.

Physically, Tanayev was an unattractive man, but he was a sensitive musician whose playing moved his audience. Tolstoy was even moved to tears when he heard him play Mendelssohn. When Sonya became obviously infatuated with the musician and began dressing for him, flirting with him, visiting him in Moscow, going to his concerts, and inviting him back to Yasnaya Polyana, Tolstoy alternately stormed and raged, or tried to use his new Christian discipline to suppress his jealously. But it was to no avail; he was jealous and humiliated, and Sonya's continuing infatuation only alienated Tolstoy more from her and from sensuality in general. "The inconsistency between my life and my beliefs," he wrote in July 1897, in a letter he never sent to Sonya:

> has long been tormenting me. . . . [N]ow I am . . . unable to go on as I have done these past sixteen years, either struggling and irritating you [and the children] or succumbing in turn to the temptations that surround me. . . . Therefore, I have . . . decided to do what I have been wanting to do for some time: leave. . . . [J]ust as the Hindus retire to the forest at the age of sixty, so any elderly religious man hopes to devote the last years of his life to God and not to pleasantries, punning, gossip and tennis matches; and so I, on the eve of my seventieth year, aspire with all my heart and soul to peace and solitude and, if not a perfect harmony between my life and conscience, at least something other than this howling clash between them. . . . Farewell, dear Sonya.

But Tolstoy did not leave—yet. Tanayev did depart, although it was not the last time Sonya would see him. Tanayev helped her endure the emotional deprivation caused by Tolstoy's ascetic Christian beliefs and allowed her to find another object of devotion, which she desperately needed. She wrote in her diary that she was "proud to have her name associated with" Tanayev, and that she had "uncrowned" Tolstoy, although she was still "profoundly attached to him."

In the midst of turmoil over Tanayev, Tolstoy wrote that "It is infinitely sad and humiliating that an utterly useless and uninteresting outsider should now be ruling our life and poisoning our last years together; infinitely sad and humiliating to be obliged to inquire when he is leaving, where he is going . . . horrible, base and shameful!" These were words Sonya could have written a few years later about Tolstoy's relationship with Chertkov, who was more than a disciple. He skillfully insinuated himself into Tolstoy's household and his confidence and replaced Sonya in Tolstoy's heart as the person with whom he shared his work and his heart. He gave Chertkov his notebooks and his copyrights as well as his affection.

Sonya wrote in her diary:

> He is all that separates us. . . . I am uncontrollably jealous of [Chertkov]; . . . I feel that he has taken from me all I have lived on for forty-eight years. . . . now I am completely left to one side. . . . No one will know I died of grief at losing my husband's love of and jealousy towards another man.

For both Sonya and Chertkov, possessing Tolstoy's diaries meant possessing Tolstoy himself. Sonya had read them since before their marriage, when he first traumatized her with his accounts of debauchery. She had copied them since and guarded them since. Now, with the advent of Chertkov, she was no longer their custodian; the diaries were entrusted to him. To

Sonya's distress, Tolstoy also named him his principle literary executor. When Sonya asserted her right to know where the diaries he had given to Chertkov were "because I am your wife, the person closest to you," Tolstoy retorted in anger, "Chertkov is the person closest to me."

nine

Last Years

During the last decade of his life, Tolstoy exercised a tremendous influence in Russia and beyond. Disciples of his religious beliefs, called Tolstoyans, formed colonies and tried to live as he prescribed. Prolific and fearless, Tolstoy wrote with the energy of a young man, even as his health failed. In 1902 he suffered a severe inflammation of the lungs. Addressing the tsar that year as "Dear Brother," Tolstoy warned him of the "evil" he would bring if he continued on the path he had taken. "Autocracy is an outmoded form of government" that can only prevail "by means of every kind of violence. . . . Measures of coercion make it possible to oppress a people but not to govern them. . . . In order [to govern] it is . . . necessary to let [the people] express their wishes and needs" and "to fulfill those which answer to the demands of . . . the mass of working people," he wrote. The

LUSTIGE BLÄTTER

Excommunicirt!

This flier depicts the excommunication of Tolstoy by the Russian Orthodox Church.

tsar ignored the letter and responded only that Tolstoy "should not worry for [the tsar] would not show it to anybody."

As innocuous, and even comical, as the tsar's response seems, it was actually sinister. His promise to "not show it to anybody" hinted that if word got out about Tolstoy's criticism of the tsar he would have no choice but to move against him somehow. It illustrates how far on the edge of acceptable behavior in the very oppressive tsarist regime Tolstoy was by the first decade of the twentieth century. A year earlier he had been excommunicated by the Russian Orthodox Church. Undercover tsarist agents spied on him, even when he was on his estate. A continuous government propaganda campaign depicted him as a revolutionary and enemy of the state, and many of his followers were exiled or jailed. Chertkov was banished from Russia for political reasons and lived in England from 1897 until 1907. For his part, Tolstoy insisted he was not a revolutionary in any conventional sense.

In January 1904, in an effort to stop Russian expansion in the east, a Japanese fleet attacked Russian ships at the harbor of Port Arthur off the tip of Manchuria. When the *North American Newspaper* cabled Tolstoy, who had become world famous for his pacifism and abhorrence of nationalism—which he argued was merely a form of collective egotism—to ask which side he supported, Tolstoy responded, "I am neither for Russia nor Japan, but for the working people of both countries, who have been deceived by their governments and forced to go to war against their own good, their conscience and their religion."

Tolstoy's response to the revolutionary uprising that broke out against the tsar in 1904–1905, which he had warned the tsar about in his scorned letter, condemned the tyranny of the government as well as the violence of the revolutionaries. "There is as much difference" between the killing that a revolutionist does and that which a government policeman does, Tolstoy responded when asked to discriminate between the two, "as between cat-shit and dog-shit. But I don't like the smell of either one or the other." The only way to attain real change and social justice was "the religious and moral perfection of all individuals." Of parliamentary reform, he wrote, "To ask me what I think about parliamentary government is like asking . . . some monk how prostitution ought to be regulated."

Although the revolutionary uprising of 1905 had failed and there had been a repressive reaction to it, Russia remained in a state of chaos that would eventually culminate in the Communist Revolution of 1917.

In 1908, Tolstoy wrote an article entitled "I Cannot Be Silent" after reading a newspaper report that the tsar's government had

Tolstoy sits at a desk in his study. *(Library of Congress)*

publicly executed twenty armed peasants for trespassing in Elizavetgrad. The article claimed that such executions were done for the good of the Russian people. "I write this and will circulate it by all means in my power both in Russia and abroad . . . either that these inhuman deeds may be stopped, or that I [be] put in prison, where I may be clearly conscious that these horrors are not committed on my behalf."

A lesser but similar horror occurred closer to home, on his property, which intensified his conflict with his wife and convinced him he had to leave Yasnaya Polyana. Even after the 1905 revolt was put down, the violence continued. Sonya's brother, Vyacheslav Behrs, was murdered by unemployed workers in St. Petersburg; peasants on the farm of Tolstoy's son Michael burned down barns housing farm machinery; on neighboring properties, prowlers shot and killed house servants and set fires. Even at Yasnaya Polyana the vegetable

Tolstoy's relationship with Sonya became strained during his later years, but she remained a devoted wife until his death in 1910.

gardens were often plundered, a night watchman was shot at, and peasants cut down more than a hundred trees for firewood. Advised by their son, Andrei, Sonya did something Tolstoy found unacceptable. She asked the governor of the province for help, and he sent police to raid the peasant homes in the neighboring village. They arrested some peasants and placed armed police guards at Yasnaya Polyana, even inside the house.

Tolstoy argued that the trees belonged to the peasants. He shouted at his wife, "Why can't you understand that the presence of the police who arrest and imprison peasants is intolerable to me."

"Then do you want them to shoot us here?" she cried back.

When the peasants complained to Tolstoy, he told them there was nothing he could do, that the property belonged to his wife. Sonya, however, was adamant. "I know you don't care . . . whether Yasnaya Polyana is torn to rack and ruin," she told their daughter Alexandra, who was on her father's side, just as Andrei was on hers. "But I don't have the right to talk like that: I have children."

Tolstoy thought Sonya was mouthing government propaganda. But he was unable to leave Yasnaya Polyana. "[N]ot that I so love fine food or a soft bed or the pleasure of riding horseback. . . . I cannot be the cause of a woman's unhappiness, provoke the anger of a person who is convinced she is doing her duty."

When Chertkov returned from exile in 1907 and built a house on land adjacent to Yasnaya Polyana, and became her husband's daily visitor, Sonya gave way to anger. She was bitter that they would be estranged during the last years of his life. "When his old age compelled him to give up sexual relations," which occurred shortly before his eightieth birthday, she recorded in 1901, "I did not see rising up to replace them a tranquil and tender friendship. Instead there was a total void." Chertkov was enjoying the companionship and friendship Sonya "had always so ardently desired."

Sonya filled the emotional void with the rage she directed against Chertkov, and violence against herself. She put herself through repeated tempestuous acts of self-destruction. She tossed herself into a freezing pond, ran barefoot through the snow, threw herself into a ditch, and threatened to drink a vial of opium, always in a fit of rage that occurred when Tolstoy favored Chertkov, whether it concerned publishing an essay, making his will, or visiting Chertkov's estate. Sonya's volatility and Tolstoy's commitment to sacrifice complemented each other. Frequently he raged against her only to overcome his anger and ask for her loving forgiveness. Similarly, after her outbursts she begged his forgiveness.

Despite their temporary reconciliations, Tolstoy harbored a desire to leave her and Yasnaya Polyana and assume the life of a wanderer or a monk, to seek shelter in a poor hut, engaged only in the purification of his soul. But he continued to write. Even after Tolstoy renounced his earlier books and began writing the social and religious tracts that made him a world-regarded prophet and a threat to the tsarist regime, the attraction to literature burned in him.

In the twelve months before his death he wrote several entries about literature in his diary. December 1909: "I want to begin an artistic book. But I do not begin because it is not ripe. I write only when I cannot but write." May 1910: "I must not write; I believe I have done all I can on that

Although he felt increasingly restricted by his family, Tolstoy appears to be unable to resist the charms of his granddaughter, Tanyasukhotin, in this photograph. *(Library of Congress)*

score. But I long to, terribly." In August 1910, in a letter to Chertkov, he confessed that he "wants to write . . . something artistic," but worries if "a real egg will emerge." At the end of October, Tolstoy sought "to rent a hut at Sharmardino," near the monastery of Optina-Pustyn, where he had written a great part of a later work, the novella *Haji Murad*, only a few years earlier.

Tolstoy was also reading intensively, which roused a desire to write. "Reading [French author, Guy de] Maupassant" made him long "to depict in literary form all the vulgarity of the life of the wealthy and bureaucratic classes and of the peasant workers, and to put in the midst of both groups at least one person who is spiritually alive. How it attracts me! What a great work it could be."

On July 7, 1910, as Tolstoy was preparing for bed, Sonya asked him to "promise . . . you won't ever leave me on the sly, without telling me." "I wouldn't ever do such a thing—I promise I shall never leave you. I love you," he assured her. But nothing seemed able to still the turbulence of their lives. Chertkov remained a disturbing presence, and Sonya's jealousy of him was not without foundation. However virtuous Chertkov's attempt to live a Christian life may have been, and however devoted he was to spreading Tolstoy's teachings, he was self-aggrandizing in his humility, and scheming in his behavior. Whether he bent Tolstoy to his wishes to reject Sonya, or only supported Tolstoy's internal need to defy his wife, is impossible to ascertain. But Sonya's fear that he was collecting information to publish after Tolstoy's death that would depict her as a harridan was correct. In the summer of 1910, Tolstoy promised Sonya he would ask Chertkov to give him back his journals. But before he returned them, Chertkov set his entire household to work copying passages he could use to create an unsympathetic picture of Sonya.

Tolstoy's will created even more intrigue than did his diaries. Sonya wanted the will to carry out Tolstoy's obligation, as she understood it, to his family, and to let her keep his estate, copyrights, and any unpublished works left in her control. Chertkov schemed to have Tolstoy designate him his legal literary heir with rights to edit and publish Tolstoy's post-1881 work. Chertkov had a legal will drawn up and convinced Tolstoy to sign it. He did this without Sonya's knowledge, despite Tolstoy's religious objections to legal contracts.

Tolstoy was torn between his wife and Chertkov. A sense of obligation that was rooted in a lifelong love for Sonya was countered by belief in the abolition of property rights. Chertkov, despite his character flaws, did understand and cherish Tolstoy's religious and philosophical works and shared his religious ideas. Sonya, despite her deep devotion to her husband, had never approved of his later works, nor followed Tolstoy in his beliefs.

As Tolstoy neared his end the conflict became more intense. There were fights over diaries, Chertkov, and the will. Sonya made endless demands. Tolstoy capitulated and rebelled, and finally resolved, despite the promise he had made to her, to leave Yasnaya Polyana to escape the turmoil. He wanted to find the solitude he longed for and he hoped still have time to reflect and write.

Tolstoy began his final flight on the morning of October 28, 1910. In his diary he wrote, "As on previous nights I heard the opening of doors and footsteps." Then he saw "through a crack" that there was a "light in the study." He heard Sonya "rustling" around and lit a candle in his bedroom. Seeing his light, "Sonya opened the door and came in, asking about 'my health' and expressing surprise at the light . . . she had seen in my room. My indignation and revulsion grew. . . . I couldn't go on lying there, and suddenly I took the final decision to leave."

Chertkov was also onto him, although Tolstoy did not know it. Chertkov received daily reports from Dr. Makovitsky and others who surreptitiously wrote down everything that happened or was said at Yasnaya Polyana.

Tolstoy wrote Sonya a farewell letter in which he acknowledged that "my departure will distress you." He was "sorry," but he "couldn't do otherwise." He explained, "I can't live any longer in these conditions of luxury." He asked her to "reconcile yourself to this new situation . . . and to have no unkind feelings" towards him. Should she need to get in touch with him, "tell Sasha; she will know where I am." Rather than reproaching his wife or dwelling on their turmoil, he focused on his own religious desire to do "what old men of my age commonly do: leav[e] this worldly life in order to spend the last days of my life in peace and solitude," which turned out not to be an accurate description of what his last days were like.

Tolstoy had taken his daughter, Alexandra (Sasha), her friend, Varvara Feokritova, and his doctor, Makovitsky into his confidence. A little after four in the morning, he met them downstairs while Sonya slept. They finished packing the few things he wanted to take with him, a trunk, a cloak, and a traveling rug. He gave Sasha his manuscripts for safekeeping and was then driven by coach to the train station with Dr. Makovitsky.

At the station, Tolstoy decided to go to the monastery at Optina-Pustyn and gave the coachman a note for Sasha informing her of his plans and asking her to tell Chertkov to inform the press that he had left his estate. At the train's first stop they bought a copy of the *Russkaya Slava*. The headline heralded the news that Tolstoy had left Yasnaya Polyana.

"The journey from Gorbachovo [to Optina-Pustyn] in a third-class railroad carriage packed with working people," Tolstoy noted "was very edifying and good, although I was too weak to take it in properly." He was able to carry on a spirited conversation with his fellow passengers, "peasants, bourgeois, workers, intellectuals, two Jews, and a high school girl" who took notes and even defended science when Tolstoy attacked it.

When he arrived at Optina-Pustyn, Tolstoy sent a telegram to Sasha and gave the coachman a letter for her. He told her that he did not want to see Chertkov or Sonya but that she ought to tell Chertkov that "I'm very glad and very afraid of what I've done. . . . I'll try and write down the subjects I think about and the stories that are on the tip of my pen." At the monastery in the midst of all this dislocation, at the age of eighty-two, Tolstoy finished an article he was writing against capital punishment.

Chertkov sent his secretary, Alexis Sergeyenko, to Optina-Pustyn. Sergeyenko told Tolstoy that Sonya had attempted several times to drown herself. In his diary Tolstoy wrote, "If somebody has to drown himself, it is I, not she, and I only want one thing—to be free of her, and of the falsehood, pretence, and malice which permeate her whole being." A day later he spoke more sympathetically of her to his sister, "You can't imagine the state she is in. . . . [J]ust think, it's dreadful—in the water."

Sergeyenko also reported that Sonya knew where Tolstoy was, which was not true, as Chertkov well knew. Sonya learned that Tolstoy was at Optina-Pustyn from a newspaper reporter on November 1. By then, however, Tolstoy had left to see his sister Marya, now a nun at the convent at Shamardino near the monastery. Although Marya was devoutly attached to the Russian Orthodox Church, her love for her brother was as strong as ever. After their final meeting she said of him, "I do not think he wanted to become Orthodox again, but I had hoped our Starets [the head of the religious house] would bring out in him the feeling of spiritual humility which he did not as yet possess, but which he was not far from in his last days."

Tolstoy spent the next day, October 30, 1910, making preparations to stay near Optina-Pustyn. He rented a hut near Shamardino. He also read *The Relationship of Socialism to Religion in General and Christianity in Particular,* which was written by one of his early disciples. He dictated a letter about the book to its author.

When Sasha arrived with news that Sonya had begun a search for him and was setting off for the vicinity of Optina-Pustyn, Tolstoy decided to leave. All of his children, apart from Sasha and the oldest, Sergey, thought that Tolstoy should return to Sonya, but this was impossible, as he wrote to Sonya in a letter he sent her before he set out for Novotcherkaska, where his niece lived. He was thinking of going on to the Caucasus, or perhaps the Crimea or even Bulgaria. He wrote: "Don't think that I left you because I don't love you—I love you and pity you with all my soul—but I can't do otherwise than I am doing. To return to you when you are in this state would mean for me to renounce life."

His declaration that he did not want "to renounce life" is revealing, especially when contrasted to the way he had characterized his yearning to leave Yasnaya Polyana before his departure. Then he had spoken of it as a way to divest himself of life's garments and prepare for death, but that was not what he said in his final note to his wife.

Tolstoy became obviously ill about four in the afternoon. He was on the train and warmly dressed in a cloak with a traveling rug thrown over him, but he was shivering and had a temperature of 100.6° F. By evening it had risen to 103.1°. The next stop was Astopovo, and he was taken off the train and put in the Ladies' Waiting room. Dr. Makovitsky spoke with Osolin, the stationmaster, and when Osolin learned it was Tolstoy who had fallen ill he offered his house as a refuge.

If Tolstoy had been successful in keeping his whereabouts secret from his wife for a few days, he had not been as successful with the press or the police. Newspapermen and police officers were on the train with Tolstoy and bulletins about his health were printed regularly. Soon crowds of people were flooding into the area to see him. Even the fledgling Pathé Cinema had sent a camera crew to film the events. There exists some herky-jerky black-and-white film of the events surrounding Tolstoy's death and pictures of Tolstoy on his deathbed.

Even when he knew he was dying, Tolstoy forbade Sasha to tell his family where he was or that he was ill. He did, however, ask to see Chertkov, who had devoted his life to Tolstoy and to his cause. Sasha wired Chertkov, and he arrived at Astopovo the following day.

Sonya had not been similarly summoned. She nevertheless arrived in Astopovo by train on November 2. Everyone attending Tolstoy thought she should not be allowed to see him. They feared it would be fatal to him. Sonya had to stay on the train when it was shunted onto a sidetrack. There are pictures of her standing outside the stationmaster's house at Astopovo peering in at the window.

Tolstoy's death was an international spectacle. His family and friends weren't the only ones who wanted to control the manner in which it occurred or reap from it their particular design. The Metropolitan, Anthonyi, head of the Russian Orthodox Church, sent telegrams, and members of the Orthodox clergy came in person, to try to persuade Tolstoy to return to the Church and to accept last rites. The clergy were not allowed to see him. Tolstoy had written only the year before, "I could no more return to the Church and take communion on my deathbed than I could use profanity or look at obscene pictures on my deathbed." The Russian police made plans in case there were riots after Tolstoy's death.

Tolstoy remained true to himself at the hour of his death. When Sasha asked if he would like her to fluff his pillows, he reminded her that there were many people in the world besides himself who needed care. To his son, Sergey, he spoke his last words, only partially coherent: "The truth. . . . I care a great deal. . . . How they."

Early on the morning of November 7, 1910, Sonya was allowed to enter Tolstoy's room when he was no longer conscious. She sat with him for ten minutes. "The doctors let me see my husband when he was scarcely breathing," she wrote in her autobiography, "and his eyes were shut. Very softly and gently I spoke into his ear hoping that he heard: 'I have been all the while here at Astopovo and I will love you to the end.' . . . Two deep sighs were the answer to my words. And then he became very calm." The others in the room were not so calm. They feared Tolstoy would regain consciousness, recognize Sonya, and there would be a scene. After Sonya left the room, Dr. Makovitsky called Tolstoy by name in a loud voice, moved a lighted candle before his face,

Mourners gather around Tolstoy's coffin at a memorial service.

and put some wine to his lips. Tolstoy made feint responses and then died.

When the train bearing Tolstoy's body arrived at Zaseka Station near Yasnaya Polyana, thousands of people were gathered to meet it, even though the government had ordered railroad officials not to put on extra trains. The church had ordered that no religious rites be provided for the funeral, nor could religious services anywhere memorialize his passing. The army was mobilized against any demonstrations in Tolstoy's honor; newspaper censorship was tightened; even florists were warned against inscribing any revolutionary slogans on the bands of memorial wreaths. Nevertheless, Tolstoy's portrait, framed in black, appeared on front pages across Russia. Theaters closed. In St. Petersburg the university canceled classes; pilgrims circled his coffin and knelt and sang a hymn—even the tsar sent a telegram of condolence to Tolstoy's family, and thousands followed his coffin as it was borne to the Zazak forest and buried beneath a tree.

Ilya Yefimovich Repin, a famous Russian artist, painted this portrait of Tolstoy reposed and reading in the forest.

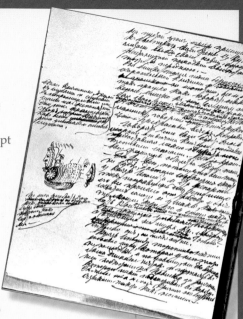

A page from the manuscript of *War and Peace* with Tolstoy's drawing in the margin *(Courtesy of Novosti/Topham/The Image Works)*

Timeline

1828: Born August 28 at Yasnaya Polyana.

1830: Mother, Marya, dies in July.

1837: Father, Nikolai Tolstoy, moves the family to Moscow in January.
June 21: Father dies; father's older sister, Aline, becomes family's legal guardian.

1838: Grandmother dies in May; family splits up; Tolstoy, ten, returns to Yasnaya Polyana under Tatanya's care, with Dmitry, eleven, and Marya, eight.

1841: Aline dies; Tolstoy and his siblings are moved to Kazan with their father's sister, Pelageya.

1845: Enters University of Kazan.

1847: Starts a diary; comes into his inheritance: 4,000 acres and 350 serfs at Yasnaya Polyana; invites Aunt